Stepping Out of It All

Stepping Out of It All

A Guide to Recovery from Everything...

CHRISTINE J. ALLEN

Library of Congress Control Number: 2021920331

HARDBACK: 978-1-956803-11-2
PAPERBACK: 978-1-956803-10-5
EBOOK: 978-1-956803-12-9

Ordering Information:

For orders and inquiries, please contact:
1-888-404-1388
www.goldtouchpress.com
book.orders@goldtouchpress.com

Printed in the United States of America

Dedicated To My Mother

Mommy --- I never thought that I could become who I am, that I'd think like I think, or have the unbelievable ability to do what I do. I never would have made it without you – without your unconditional love, faith, support, encouragement and inspiration. You inspired me to just be me. I am who I am because you believed...

This book is dedicated to my mother, Juanita, who was, by far, my biggest fan and perpetual supporter. She genuinely loved me far more than I could love myself, consistently told me that I could do anything that I put my mind to, and took great care of me until the day she died. My Mom believed I was exceptionally talented, beautiful, extraordinary, brilliant, special and amazing – long before I believed in my own gifts, talents, and abilities. Because of her belief in me, I have learned to be confident in my ability to be all that I was destined to be. I am blessed with virtuous character, integrity, substance, vision, and purpose. I am a woman of indescribable strength, fortitude, tenacity and power. I am enough! I am more than enough! I believe I am so much more today than I ever imagined I would be! Thank you for your guidance, for all of the needed care, and for loving me in ways that only a mother could.

Christine J. Allen

And God, thank you for Your Love, Your limitless Grace and unending mercy that continues to cover me. Thank you for ordering my steps according to your will and purpose for my life. Thank you for helping me to see your hand in everything I do. Thank you for all that you have done and will do for me. This book is a reality because of God's amazing grace and limitless favor…..

"Make the most of yourself.
For that is all there is of you."

--- Emerson

Foreword

I have put together all the information that I believe could serve as a basic guide to sort through some of the things that stand in the way of your potential greatness. I assure you, this book will help you in ways that you cannot imagine in this moment. What I have written has certainly helped me....

I wrote this book because I felt compelled to tell my story. I genuinely want to help others. And it makes no sense to have learned all that I learned on this incredible journey called Life, only to keep those insights and lessons all to myself. I began this work in 2008, a year after my mother passed away. I was not inspired to write again until New Year's Day of 2011, right after the tragic death of a struggling superstar. In 2012, I was motivated to finish what I started. And now, in 2021, I am revising this book to share new insights, new revelations, new awakenings, and inspiring moments that changed my life.

I've been so many different versions of myself – The Teenaged Me, The Me of my Twenties, of my Thirties, of my Forties, of my Fifties, and now, the 60-something version of myself. It's crazy because after all these years, right now, I am the best version of myself that I've ever been. I am becoming more compassionate, loving, confident, valuable, valued, self-determined, and more self-assured. I am becoming the version of woman that I always wanted to be, but didn't quite know how to be, or maybe was just too afraid to step out and be that. That's just not my story today….

I have gone through quite a lot in my life, and have had a wide range of thoughts, ideas about life, about people, places, things; reasons, rationales, assumptions, conjectures about life. And now, at this time in my life, I have experienced a miraculous transformation of my personal views, of my beliefs, my values, my perception, my perspective, and my overall philosophy about life. My vision has changed. My self-image has changed. My perception has changed. What I believe in and how I believe about myself has changed. And change just keeps happening. Maybe because I'm open to it or maybe because the season to change has come. I just know that everything that concerns me has changed. And sometimes, the changes have occurred without my permission. At other times, I made a conscious decision to do something different that caused the change to happen. But, every thing that changed was necessary. And despite my resistance to change, today I am learning to accept and embrace change as it comes. I do so, mainly, because it is less painful to accept and embrace it than it is to resist the inevitability of it. Yup….

In my life, I have self-loathed and self-loved. I have had a sense of superiority and felt deep-rooted inferiority as a result of the recurring conflict with my unpredictable ego and an unbalanced sense of self-esteem. I've had times when I valued no thing, and have experienced instances when I've felt genuinely grateful for everything. At times, I've felt hopeless and suicidal. At times, I've had deep rage and felt disturbingly homicidal. Sometimes, I felt both of those things at the same time. I have come to know that I am not alone with these feelings…

I have been absurdly self-righteous, blinded by ego and a grand sense of self. I've been, consequently, humbled by my ego and the excessive levels of pride and arrogance. I've accepted the unacceptable because I didn't feel enough self-worth to not accept it. I have loved and lost. I've been lost by that kind of loss and was left with no one to love but me. And I didn't….

I have been removed from life-threatening circumstances, and have been miraculously resurrected like a Phoenix from the dust. More than once…. I've felt low and desperate, and could not see a way out. I've heard a quiet voice in the midst of my desperation, and acted as if it was not a message specifically designed for me. I've ignored things I knew were presented to gain my attention. I've been deeply hurt by some unexpected life situations. Deeply saddening disappointments that could have broken me. And I did wonder, in anguish, why God would allow these things to happen to me. Yet now, I appreciate every one of those experiences because they shaped me, changed me, redirected and recalibrated me. Those things made me who I am today. I am grateful to have learned what I learned from those life lessons. Grateful, in retrospect, to have gotten to a place where I embrace even the not-so-nice experiences --- just for what they were and for what they meant to my personal development. Now, I recognize fully that my present life is the sum total of all those moments: the well-thought out and the irrational choices; the hurts, the fears, the failures, and the successes; every tear, every pain, every joy, every victory, every thought, every decision that I've made. I learned that it was all necessary. I have learned to embrace it all.

It was all good. It _is_ all good....

And with all of my lived experience, after all of the life-changing situations that I went through, just when I thought that my life had taken all the turns that it could, another change happened: The COVID-19 Pandemic of 2020! I started to look at my life with a spiritual microscope. My God!!! What had I done with my life? What had I actually done with all of the years that had passed? I began to recognize, through a changed lens that was altered by the reality of my own mortality, that my time, my life was getting shorter -- by the minute. I experienced a pronounced, very overwhelming fear that I was getting closer to my end. I recognized that I'd wasted so much time, obsessing over and being consumed by ridiculous, inconsequential nonsense. I had overlooked some very important moments, missed some things that I should have been paying attention to and didn't. I had focused so much time and energy on things that really didn't matter. Well, things that no longer mattered in the context of a global pandemic. I don't know when I lost my focus and went off track, but I knew that it was time to get my life in order. I began to think about the end-game: How much more time did I have? How long would I live? What had been my contributions? What would people say about me when I was gone? What would be my legacy? I began to think seriously about purpose: what is my purpose? How would I gain the courage, the focus, the fortitude and tenacity to seek out my purpose and execute as needed. And just how could I become who and what I need to achieve my purpose? Before my end…?

I had read somewhere or heard on some talk show that I have the choice to be whatever I want to be. I can choose to be sad and dissatisfied or to be happy and grateful. I have the choice to be disillusioned by the things that I don't have or the things that haven't gone my way; or I can choose to be grateful, satisfied, and inspired by the things, the gifts that I do have. I have the choice to give up my obsessions over men, money, menopause, moods, my age, my grays, my love life (or lack thereof), and all of the stuff that had taken my attention hostage. I can choose. I have the freedom of choice. I can decide how I want to live. I can choose what and who I want to be. I can choose to believe that I am not worthy or that I'm worth more than I've believed over the span of my years. I can choose to love myself more, to love myself better, and I am responsible for treating myself as if I do. I can choose to believe that I am enough --- that I am more than enough --- just as I am. They said that I could redefine my path, re-envision my reality, course correct, create my own success, and build what I want to see for myself. I could choose to accept myself --- just as I am. I could choose to be my own *happily ever after*, despite the unforeseen, unexpected life stuff, despite my reality as it is. I could choose to believe that there could be more to life, more to my life, more to me, more in me. That's what they said. I have a choice. I could choose. So, I did.

I'm a thinker. I'm always thinking about stuff: why, what, when, how, who, what if, maybe if, if only…. You get the picture. Always thinking! And sometimes, it's difficult to look at my life for what it was and for what it is without a warped perspective. And it has been equally as painful to share my thoughts with others. I don't always like to talk about the choices that I've made, the ones that I didn't, the opportunities that I missed, the ones I took advantage of, the parts of my life that continue to be, the damaged parts of me that I'm working on, the pieces of me that no longer exist. And though some choices that I made left me feeling angry, sad, ashamed, apprehensive, disgusted, humiliated, embarrassed, remorseful and confused, I recognize that every choice and experience was critical to my life now. So, I am learning to accept and embrace my reality. All of it….

And I can say, for the most part, that I am pleased with changes that I've made, with the course that I've taken, and am loving the person that I am becoming. I am really pleased with how things are turning out. I'm learning and listening. I'm paying attention. To me. To everything! And I keep on living, each day, with renewed zeal, intention and focus. I am living, living out loud, with confidence, faith, trust and hope. In God and in me. And I can say, with a real sense of certainty, that "It's all good."

In retrospect, I understand what did and didn't happen, and can even see why some things that happened had to happen for me exactly as they did. I really wish that I knew then what I know now. But, I didn't. I had to find a way to accept reality as it is, to accept me as I am, to acknowledge missteps and mistakes, and to forgive myself. Had to figure out how to get up, brush myself off, get a Plan B, keep moving forward, and do all that I can to attain the success that I envision. I will say that my life, as it is, would not have been possible without developing a distinct ability to accept, endure, reflect, understand, and make the necessary adjustments, and keep moving. I accept all of it! The past and present, good, bad and ugly; the achievements and successes, the losses and failures, the unthinkable, life-changing moments. I accept the role that all of those things played. They are all a part of my spiritual fabric. I am committed to "being good" with who I am. ALL of who I am. Are you?

I am a survivor! I am a survivor of a functioning dysfunctional alcoholic household; of overrated middle-classism; of reciprocal marital/domestic violence; of unexpected infidelity; of excessive drinking, uncontrolled drugging and long-term chain-smoking; of unconsciously eating all of my feelings; of not having enough; of feeling like I was not enough; of overachieving for all the wrong reasons; of looking for love in all the wrong places; of a broken marriage; of a broken heart; of abandonment by all of the men in my life; of the need to be loved, way too much; of no self-worth and damaged self-esteem; of lack of confidence; of a flawed self-image; of a broken/fractured personality; of needing validation; of unrelenting loneliness; of a tattoo-infused mid-life crisis; of a multitude of spiritual and emotional disorders. I am a survivor of so many things that have periodically overwhelmed me throughout the years, some that have troubled me for all of my life. But, the point is --- I am a survivor!

I'm a survivor, recovering from decades of living uncomfortably with myself. I've always been uncomfortable being in my own skin, while trying to be comfortable with everyone else. I am recovering from a number of isms, schisms, ideologies and views, from unfounded ideas, beliefs and attitudes, distressing obsessions, irrational thinking, and unhealthy behaviors. I am recovering from a lot of things, a duffel bag full of life concerns. What's most important to say is, I am recovering from myself. Uh huh….

I am a recovering woman --- recovering from an inability to deal with the truth. I am recovering from fantasy; from grandiosity; from failures; from fear of failure; from self-centered fear; from low self-worth and people-pleasing to prove my worth; from lying to myself and lying to others; from illusion and delusion; from an inability to confront; from running away; from not standing up; from moving too fast; from moving too slow; from just being stuck, with no idea how to move and nowhere to go. I am recovering from myriad emotions – from feelings; hurt feelings; from unresolved anger and long-term resentments, from on-going frustrations; from disheartening disillusionment. I am recovering from love – from not getting enough and not getting what I need; from giving too much; from heartache and heartbreak; from pain -- emotional, physical, mental, spiritual; from self-indulgence based in pain; from too much of a bunch of stuff used to mask the pain; from self-neglect; from negative self-perception; from skewed perceptions of others; from very distorted thinking; from being trapped inside my own thinking, stuck inside of my own mind, confined by my own self-imposed prison – struggling and grappling to get myself out. Unfree….

I am recovering from all of that. I am learning how to navigate and survive my emotions, and am working to change outdated approaches that I've used to manage life as it presents. I am a woman in the process of recovery. I am slowly recovering. Slowly, but surely…. I am working it out!

Please don't stop reading because I use the word "recovery". Webster's New World dictionary defines *recovery* as "a return to health; a regaining of one's balance." To *recover* is "to get back something lost; to regain health, balance, or control; to save oneself from a fall; to reclaim; to make up for, to recover what was lost". My belief in the practice and philosophy of recovery has saved me from so many things. My life has been changed, and I was saved by the idea that I could recover. The idea that I could get better, be better and do better. It was the principles of recovery that slowly guided me to a better version of myself.

So, my mission and purpose is to share with others how they can use the concepts of recovery to get better. My goal is to support others in their personal process of getting comfortable with themselves, to become more comfortable with others, and ultimately, to be more comfortable dealing with life. I want to share the viable, valuable truths that I discovered, the greatest of which is "It is possible to recover." It is possible to recover --- from anything!! From everything….

I have also learned, just by living amongst other people, that everybody has issues. Everybody is dealing with some *thing*. Everybody is trying to get over or through some thing, trying to move successfully toward something else. And each of us is trying to maintain some semblance of sanity while doing that. Learning to do that is what recovery is all about. Moving forward without the weight of baggage from the past weighing you down is what recovery is about. Learning how to move away and stay away from things of the past, or to deal more healthily when those things arise is what recovery is all about. Managing your reality – the struggle and juggle of all of it – is what recovery is about. Finding a better way to live your life is what recovery is all about. Finding the best way to be the best version of you, by changing what no longer serves you, is what recovery is about. Finding balance, peace and a realistic view of self is what recovering people do. I am a recovering person. That is what I do. And you can recover, too. So, come on now. Keep reading….

And as you read about what I have learned about me, you will recognize some things that you may (or may not) know <u>and</u> accept about you. This book will give you information to help you to examine yourself honestly, to sort through all of the noise, and through the confusion and contradictions that you find throughout the process. This book will help you to develop an approach, a strategy, a recipe, a plan to move from any Point A (issue/problem) to its respective Point B (outcome/solution).

I will share my truth to help you to understand why it is so important to identify and accept your truth --- for yourself. You will gain some new insights and maybe revisit old ideas about how the process of change works. If you're open, you will have an opportunity to move forward toward who, how, what, and where you want to be in your life. I guarantee that you will be inspired to do the work, to do your work; to develop awareness and acceptance, and determine what you need to do to be your best self. Through your own efforts…..

I've done lots of introspection and reflection. I've made conscious decisions to do what was needed to redefine myself. I write this to encourage folks who have been brought to their knees by life concerns, experiences, issues, situations, problems and/or people. This book is for those who have fallen down (or who've been brought down), and can't seem to get back up. It is for anyone who wants to get back on track. I'm writing this for any person who wants to find a new way to be, to think, to act, to live. I write this for anyone who thinks you're the only one going through what you're going through. You're not… Really! I write this for folks who need a breakthrough; for those who desire a mental, emotional, and/or spiritual makeover. I've created this book as a guide to recover. This is a very simple step-by-step blueprint for change. I want to share an ideology that has helped tens of thousands. It has certainly helped me to gain a better perspective on my life, and improved my ability to navigate life while living it.

I woke up one day and was in my mid-fifties. I decided that I wanted a different kind of life for myself. I realized I had spent a great part of my life, way too much time, going through the motions and just being ordinary. You know, living an ordinary, uneventful, lackluster existence. I was grateful for what I had, but I wanted more. I believed I could attain more if I became willing to do more to get more of what I wanted. I have become more than ordinary because of that revelation. I have, through focused attention and improved perspectives on everything, transformed my thinking, improved my be-ing, and created an extraordinary life for myself. I am writing this book because that is an extraordinary thing to do. I believed that I could and should do it, so I did. I am extraordinary. I am…. Actually, I am a phenomenal and amazing woman as a result of the recovery process! I have experienced a profound evolution from the woman I was to the woman I am. I am still in the midst of my transformation. And you can do it, too.

This is the key point that I want to make – that if I can change, develop, improve, transform, and recover from the laundry list of life stuff that kept me stuck for so long, you can recover from your life stuff, too! No really, you can….

So, how did this change occur for me, you ask? Well, the journey of change began with me. It began with a desire to change. It began with me becoming honest with myself, open-minded to the ideas of others, and willing to change what needed to change, despite the fear that accompanied the idea of change. It began with me taking a look at my thinking --- my thoughts, my ideas, my perception and perspective --- because my thinking always drove my behavior. What and how I thought dictated what I did in response to my thoughts. It still does. My thinking is the foundation from which my behavior derives. So, I learned how to pay attention to my thinking. I learned how to pay close attention to "what came next" in a situation. I learned to monitor my thinking, my feelings, my attitude, my triggers, my mood swings, and behaviors that corresponded with those things. I learned how to pay attention to everything that I did. I learned to ask myself questions: "Why are you doing that? Why are you saying that? Why did you respond like that? What are you feeling? Why do you feel like that? What is the exact nature of those feelings? Why do you feel like that now? Why does that person/situation create those feelings in you? Why do you react like that to that? Why are you doing *that* again? What do you need? What don't you have? What's really going on with you? I learned how to keep myself under observation. You know why? Because

I discovered that I need to be observed, monitored, watched, and kept under surveillance. 24/7. By me. At all times. No, seriously….

And once I learned the importance of monitoring and honestly examining myself *in real time*, I began to monitor and examine others, especially people who I'd allowed into my life. I looked at all of the relationships that I'd developed, the nature of each relationship (intimate/love interests, family, friends, colleagues, and casual acquaintances). I began to look at the value of each relationship – what each relationship meant to me; why I was in it or no longer in it; what caused it to work or caused it to not work anymore; if the cause was me or if it was not; how I could change it or what could be done if it could not be changed; when a relationship was over; how did it end and why it was over; why did I stay, even when it was over; why I'd held on; why I wouldn't let go; why I held on so tightly, even if the pain of holding on was killing me, and not so softly…. I learned how to get relief, how to keep myself from going insane from the intensity of foolishness that pervaded the relationship. I found out that I could walk away – but, only if I monitored me when I was going in and was honest about it while in it. I found that I could retain my mental, emotional and spiritual equilibrium, if I paid attention. I learned how to find my way back to myself, if I began to lose myself in any relationship. I learned that I was responsible for defining and honoring my own needs, feelings and expectations when involved with another person. But, first I had to understand 'who I am' and 'what I need' before I could present expectations for someone else to meet. I learned how to do that and other things that empowered me to be the woman I wanted to be in relation to others. And somewhere in the process of change, I began to place more appropriate worth and value on the most significant relationship that I would have – the one with my self. And that's where the real work began…

Through understanding and developing a better relationship with my self, I came to believe that everything begins and ends with me. I am keenly aware of how my mental/emotional state and my spiritual condition directly affect everything. When I am good with me, and clear about who I am, where I am, what I feel, what's going on here, how I'm feeling about what's going on, <u>and</u> have tapped into my spiritual tools, I am so much better with everyone and everything around me. But, when I'm not good with me, when there's something out of order or I'm ignoring or unaware that something is out of order, I begin to move carelessly, in and out of consciousness, flailing, moving recklessly on an unsafe collision course with everyone around me. And that has never ended well!! I know that I am responsible for my behavior. I learned that I can manage my behavior, when I am aware of and attentive to my thinking. Hmmm…

So, how do we change our thinking? Our life-long perspectives? Our old ideas and attitudes? Our ideologies? Our core values? Our belief system? Just how do we change how and what we think? And how do we change what we do? How do we change the way that we've always been, how we've always dealt with people, problems, challenges, situations, issues, circumstances, and everything else?

Well, in order to initiate change, you must be willing to change. But even before that, you have to be open-minded and willing to get honest – with you. You know, the practice of self-honesty. Can you be honest with you? Can you tell yourself the truth? Because it is only through self-honesty that you can begin to recognize and accept who you are – your thoughts, attitudes, likes and dislikes, biases, assets, defects, emotions, triggers, traumas, distorted thought processes, and lies you've told yourself. You have to get honest about all of that. And you'll need to get really honest about your secrets -- those little, dark secrets that you think about, but don't talk about because of fear, shame, guilt and remorse – those things that have continually driven you with powerful force, usually against your will…. Yeah. Change can only occur when you can get honest about what is.

As you begin to take an honest look at yourself, you will be able to identify why you are who you are and why you do what you do. You'll learn how get honest about yourself to yourself, and that will be a critical starting point in your recovery process. And no, it will not happen overnight because humans aren't wired like that. We are conditioned to do what we've always done, and we will do what we do over and over again, despite the consequences. How we think and what we do becomes a part of us. And even though higher intellect provides us an out, we usually don't take it. Freedom of choice and free will and rational, logical thinking --- the higher intellectual functions of human beings -- affords us the capacity to make good decisions and do something different. But, we don't. Not without a conscious effort. Not without a fight. Nope. Our patterns and emotions tend to get in the way. Our feelings often defy our logic and intellect. Feelings can make us do peculiar things, often against our own wills. Many undesired behaviors occur over and over again, until the discomfort of doing those things begins to compel us to look at ourselves honestly. And that doesn't happen until it's time for it to happen. Have you ever been sick and tired of being sick and tired of yourself? Uh huh. I'm sure….

They say "You can't teach an old dog new tricks" but I beg to differ. I, metaphorically, am an old dog who has learned many new tricks. And I continue to be open to learn some new thing each day. I take the opportunity to learn when I can because that practice has led to real transformative change. I changed because I needed to. I stay open to the idea of change because I recognize that there is always something that could be better. I long to change because the benefits of changing outweigh the desire to stay the same. Achieving one's own desired level of *extraordinary* requires that one continues to make the effort to be better. There is always better. There is always an opportunity to be better and to do better. I achieve the desired outcomes in my life only when I am honest with me and when I am willing to make the effort to get what I want.

The truth is, change can happen for anyone. We can recondition ourselves, recondition how we think and change what we do in response to what we think. If we have the desire to change. Desire will ignite change. Commitment will drive it. If you have a desire to respond to life in a different way, to live your life in a different way, take this opportunity to make a commitment to do some things differently. You can create a new life. You can define and achieve anything that you want. You can change. You can recover!!

Check out how it worked for me….

What Had Happened Was...

I was introduced to recovery through a self-help program after I'd lost control of my life back in the 90's. I am a product of the 60's and 70's. I was a very bright, loving, happy, middle-class fat girl – a kind of geeky, overachieving teacher's pet type – who wanted to be down. I was obedient at home and in school. I was a great student because the better the grades, the better the stuff they bought for me – shoes and clothes and stuff. I was a good girl because I wanted acceptance from my parents and teachers. But secretly, I needed acceptance from my peers. And that wasn't happening because I was labelled a "smarty, goody-two-shoes" and I hated it. It kept me in a box that really separated me from the people who were fun and didn't care about what others thought. That labelling continued for me from elementary school until high school. And then, everything began to change.…

I wanted to be down with the cool kids. The cool kids drank a little and did "light" drugs (a few joints here and there). In the 70's, we drank wine coolers, Pink Champale, Boone's Farm wine and Sangria, on the sly. We smoked reefer at the latch-key kids' houses during or after school, and went to house parties on the weekends. Well, hanging with them made me a part of --- doing drugs got me in with the "in crowd", and being "in" superseded logic and everything that I knew to be true at the time. In the 80's, many of my crowd went on to college by day, and smoked weed, sniffed cocaine, and went drinking and dancing at night. I continued to use drugs because that's what college kids did. I was unconsciously driven by the continued need for acceptance and an unconscious peer pressure. We call it people-pleasing now. Most of us graduated – some from college, some to free-basing. I did both. Later in the 80's, we began to smoke cocaine cigarettes because it was the thing of the times and what being a part of the crowd dictated. That social drug use led me to smoke crack-cocaine – the next step in the progression of drug use for a lot of 80's cocaine users. We got involved with crack because we didn't understand the nature of the drug or the power of addiction. We continued to use because we didn't understand the nature of addiction nor did we recognize that we couldn't stop using even if we wanted to. Most of us didn't realize didn't realize until it was too late! Some of my friends stopped using at some point. It got to be too much. Using became too ugly, too dirty, too consuming, too scary. But, I did not. I could not and I really didn't understand why.…

By the early 90's, drugs had caused a lot of good people to fall victim to the nasty, downward spiral of addiction. We were using drugs against our wills, and weren't aware of the fact that the disease of addiction had overtaken our normal thinking and living. Addiction is a cunning, baffling, insidious, aggressively destructive power. It was overpowering us. We didn't know that there was a line to be crossed until we'd crossed it. We just didn't know. And when we were at the point that we could see the outward destruction, the deterioration, the losses, and the wreckage from the subculture lifestyle, it was too late to save ourselves from ourselves. And many of us still couldn't see the physical, mental, emotional, physiological and spiritual damage that was being done, until we were too far gone to do anything about it. We didn't understand some of it, and were unaware or in denial about the rest. We just couldn't see ourselves as we were. Many of us who had been productive contributors, law-abiding, working-class, thriving family men and women, had transformed into untrustworthy, unpredictable, unreliable, hopeless, drug-addicted shells of our former selves. I had lost the ability to stop using, and was on the path to losing myself.

By the mid-90's, drug addiction had me locked in a vicious cycle of using – I used drugs because I felt bad and I felt bad because I used drugs, and used drugs because I felt bad… You get the idea. I neglected my child, intimidated my mother, disgraced my family, lost some jobs, and jeopardized everything that was important to me. It was a terrifying time for me. I was dying physically and spiritually. My life had become an endless loop of horrifying experiences. Drug addiction forced me into a dark place, and I was compelled to seek help or die an ugly death. Fortunately, I was able to get the help I needed before I'd lost myself forever. The help I found led me to treatment, and that led me to a Twelve Step recovery program, based primarily on the idea that you must help yourself if you want to get better. I learned how to help myself, after learning how to ask for help. Eventually, I got better….

Twelve Step programs are self-help programs that provide very practical approaches and strategies that are grounded in both therapeutic counseling models and spiritual principles, supported by structured guidelines for improved living. And those guidelines support a person's desire to change behaviors in order to experience better outcomes. The effectiveness of these programs is based primarily on one's commitment to do something different in order to get something different. The self-help approach is a method that has helped thousands of individuals to help themselves with various issues. Twelve Step programs can provide supportive networks of other people who have common issues to address and overcome. The recovery process offers opportunities to change attitudes, thinking and behaviors, and create a new path for your life. Just keep reading....

As I continued to receive support and assistance from members of various groups, I began to achieve considerable 'clean time' – time away from the drug use. But, as I began to clear up from the drugs, I started to realize that I needed to address some issues that had affected the quality of my clean living. And that was the point that I began to actively utilize the principles of recovery to address those concerns so I could recover from my self. After the drugs were gone, I was left with a better view of who I was. And I wasn't happy. The need for change became more and more apparent to me, as I stayed clean and began to pay attention to myself. Through the recovery process, I began to learn about how to change, a key component of my success with abstinence. The process of recovery dramatically changed my life. It kept me away from the drugs, but there was so much more that I gained other than sustained abstinence from drugs. The longer I practiced recovery principles and was willing to engage in personal introspective work, the more I realized that recovery was essential, not only to continued abstinence, but to a more successful way of living. I recognized that in order to create and maintain the changes desired, I would have to continue to do what I had done in the early stage of recovery – get honest, be open, become willing, and have a desire. I found that when I applied recovery principles to other areas of my life, I began to experience the changes needed in those areas, too. I began to apply the principles of recovery to everything. And, when I did, a great transformation began to happen. I began to change everything….

I talk to people all the time – and not just to people in recovery. I like to talk to any and everybody. We talk about life, love, faith, hope, about being more, being better; about defining goals and attaining our versions of success; about spiritual perspective and spiritual condition, about God and our understanding of God; about people and their behaviors; how to deal with people more effectively; dealing with children, especially the grown ones; surviving the "empty nest" syndrome; dealing with exes - divorced husbands and old boyfriends; about how to manage ourselves and manage our emotions; about getting older; being wiser; being kinder; finding peace; chasing dreams at this stage of life; career changes and life planning; and pursuing vision of a joyous life. And when I talk to 'regular' people, I realize that they want and need the same things that I, a recovering person, wants and needs. I also realize that they need some of the same life lessons that recovery has afforded me. They want and need what I have to offer. And I want nothing more than to share what I have learned with them. The confidence that they see and the successes that I've achieved are, in essence, all a result of working a recovery program.

Most 12-step recovery programs are based on an identifiable issue that has become problematic – alcohol, drugs, sex, food, gambling, etc. So, if an individual does not have a distinct issue embodied by a 12-step program, it stands to reason that s/he will most probably not seek out the support available from an existing 12-step program. And that's where the vital information contained in this book comes in…..

We, in my particular 12-Step recovery program, have continually believed that we should find ways to share the idea of recovery with the rest of the world. We wish we could tell the world how good recovery is, and the incredible effects that it can have on one's life, without breaking our own anonymity. We talk about sharing about the power of a life built on the foundation of spiritual principles, without compromising the integrity of our anonymous program.

I know that I have been supportive to a lot people with their life issues, by sharing experiences about the results of practicing a strong recovery program. It has helped me with my issues. I am cognizant that the ideology of the 12-step program is a treasure chest filled with practical information that can help people, all people, to get better. But, the "unaffected" don't, won't or refuse to believe that recovery can apply to them.

I believe, from my experience, that the recovery process can be valuable for anyone who wants to change. Why do I believe? Because I've seen it happen for people who are connected to people who understand and share the process with them. I learned that issues are the same. Why? Because all issues are people issues….. Whether you're a recovering addict dealing with relationship issues or a non-addicted person dealing with relationship issues, it's the same. The pain is the same. The feelings are the same. We're all the same. The goal is the same – to successfully navigate through the problem, find a solution, and get relief from the unbearable pain. It's all the same….

And though I have taken every precaution to keep specific aspects of my 12-Step program anonymous, I am going to take a risk in an effort to share my truth – the lessons and strategies that I gained from recovery – to help you with your life changes.

So, I want to identify the areas of my life that have changed as a result of integrating the use of recovery principles into my life:

- My understanding of Addiction (& Recovery)
- Drug Dependency
- Alcohol Dependency
- Food Addiction – what that relationship means to me
- Loss of Love – what being alone means to me
- Broken Relationships / Divorce survivor – the impact
- New Relationships – What having a man means to me
- All Friendships – What being a friend means to me
- Lying, Cheating, Stealing (all under the same umbrella)
- Death / Grief / Trauma survivor
- Abandonment issues
- Self-Image / Self-Worth / Self-Confidence / Self-Esteem
- Old Attitudes and Bad Behaviors
- Motherhood / Parenting grown children
- Finances / Self-Sufficiency
- Social Status (what I need and don't need from it)
- Spiritual Development

Now, please don't try to convince yourself that this information will not help you. And please don't resist the desire to follow the guidance offered because of the idea that you don't need help. Stop it! Everybody needs help. It takes a village to live and learn and thrive and succeed, whether you believe it or not! Get the help and support that you need from this book. I can attest that these things that I share can and will change your life.

Get into it. Go with it! Lean in….

Take a risk and see what happens.

Take a chance and maybe you will begin to recover too….

How I Got To Here...

I was married for most of my adult life. I got married one month after graduating from college. I was 22 years old, I hadn't been anywhere, hadn't travelled anywhere, hadn't seen anything, nor had I done anything out of the ordinary for the early part of my life. I went to college and made a plan to get out of my parents' house as soon as I could. Me and my husband were young and clueless, unfocused, ill-prepared, and were not ready for the marriage experience. We had no real plans and no direction. We were friends from high school who liked each other. During college, we got into a serious relationship, and began to have sex and get high with each other. We thought getting married would allow us a freedom to have our own place, where we could live and just be (unsupervised), have long, loud, hot, frequent sex when we felt like it (out from under the listening ear of my Daddy), and get high whenever we wanted (out from under the watchful eye of my Mommy). In hindsight, I believe someone should have stopped or slowed us down with the marriage talk. Someone (a parent, relative, friend, somebody) with some wisdom and insight (who we probably wouldn't have listened to anyway) should have slowed the speed at which our plans to marry were moving. But, that didn't happen. So, we were two not-fully-grown adults who got married. We had no idea what being married entailed, nor did we have the spiritual maturity or personal commitment to do all that was needed to sustain a marriage. We didn't know what grown people did to maintain a household, how they managed the finances, how they planned for the future, or how they created effective approaches to cooperation, collaboration and communication that both parties could understand. We played house as best we could, we worked because we knew we should, we argued frequently, listened rarely, and volleyed often in the effort to win in the game of Marital Power Play. We acted like we knew what we were doing. And it was not that bad. For a while….

The drug use progressed over a period of time and began to noticeably affect us. We got messy and careless regarding the normal things that needed attention. And as the pressures to perform and maintain responsibilities increased, our ability to handle it all decreased. Things really began to get worse fast. We used drugs to mask the pain of our failure and inadequacy, and to numb the feelings of guilt, shame, and embarrassment. We were making a mess of our lives and we couldn't stop it. At some point, I realized I was pregnant. It was God's miraculous grace that, for most of my pregnancy, we did not use drugs. We knew that that was wrong on so many different levels. We were blessed to stay clean and lived as a normal, expectant couple. But, just like with the marriage, we were ill-equipped and had no idea what being parents required. When my son was born, we were not ready for it. Life became increasingly challenging very quickly, and shortly after my son's birth, we began to use drugs 'socially' again.

There is so much that happened in such a short time. We couldn't explain why our life as it was — as new working parents with so many possibilities to be successful — was not enough. Our lives quickly began to spiral out of control and we spun wildly down to new levels of using. We put everything at risk and we couldn't see it. We were reckless with everything and gave very little care to the things that should have mattered. It was our grace that we had mothers / families who were deeply concerned about us, very involved in our lives, and had enough love and care to give to our son in our periods of absence. The Family stepped in and took the opportunity to nurture our son, while we spent a great deal of time away from home and from him on intermittent drug binges. We'd stop using for a while, but we'd always go back. We were caught in the vicious cycle of addiction and we just didn't know how to get out….

After what I now know was a family intervention, we were both sent to drug treatment programs to get ourselves together. I spent a short time in a New York program and was introduced to the idea of recovery at that facility. My husband went to several treatment programs because he continued to use after release. Ultimately, my great plan was to get clean and stay clean, then, I could help him to get clean and stay clean. I found out that that was not an effective plan. Why? Because recovery doesn't work like that. I was able to show him how recovery was working for me, but I could not ignite his flame of desire to stay clean. So, while he used drugs, spent a lot of time at parties and clubs, and found pleasure in the company of other women, I suffered in silence and told no one about the pain that I was in. I knew I needed to stay close to the people in 12-Step recovery meetings, but I did not understand how important it was for me to talk about my feelings. I was just trying to stay clean and not kill myself because of the pain, the shame and anguish of it all. I had been able, through grace, desire and willingness, to build a solid recovery foundation. The program was definitely working because in the midst of this crisis, I was not using. I prayed and held on, waiting for him to recognize how good recovery was, and to realize that we could "live happily ever after" if he would just stop using drugs and be my husband. But, he did neither. Well, not at first…..

My husband used off and on for the first year of my recovery. And then, he got clean. And we stayed clean together for about two years. Then, he relapsed and kept using drugs for another two years. I wanted him clean because I knew what a good man he was. I could envision the good life that we could have doing recovery together. I wanted to help him to get clean and stay clean. But, my recovery friends consistently reminded me that you can carry the message, but you cannot carry the addict. We can only help someone who wants to be helped. And he was not yet ready for the help that we were offering…. A few days before my 40th birthday, he left. He left me because I gave him a choice, an ultimatum really, to change or to leave. He knew he was not ready to change, so he chose to leave. And when he left, a part of me left with him. He abandoned me. He left me and my son. But what really shocked me was that I abandoned myself for a while, too. And it took a lot of time and work to heal and return to myself.

Back in the 70's, I had gone to see an Off Broadway play called *For Colored Girls Who Have Considered Suicide When the Rainbow Was Not Enough*. I didn't realize, when we'd first separated, why scenes from the play kept coming back to mind, I, later, realized that those recurring scenes came to me because I had begun to consider my own suicide to end the unbearable pain of living without him. I started to understand what those women were portraying in that play, many years before. And of all the segments in *For Colored Girls*, what stuck out in my mind was the scene with a woman who talked about her man "walking away with all of her stuff". For the first time, I knew exactly what she meant. I felt like he had walked away with all of my stuff --- he had taken all of the essence of me when he left. I had unintentionally surrendered myself over to him, and felt I had nothing left of me when he walked out the door.

I had only wanted to be a wife, his wife. And without him, I felt I had no value or purpose; I was a non-entity with, a non-entity with nothing left to live for. I had lost myself, lost my identity, lost my sense of self, lost the essence of who I was, sacrificed parts of me that I needed to be my self. I had given up parts that were necessary, important, of value to me, before he came along. I was indistinguishable – couldn't separate where I ended and where he began. Wasn't able to identify what was me and what was him. I had mutated into a part of him, so there was no real need for me to exist. That's really how I felt…. I had no desire to continue living when he walked away. I wanted to die and I didn't know how to get back to wanting to live again. I'd lost my best friend, my life partner, my person. I didn't understand how he could just leave like that. I assumed that he would only be able to walk away without a fight like that because I was not worth it. I was not worth fighting for. I was not worth fighting for? Our marriage was not worth fighting for? I could not figure out how to want to go on living with the pain and shame caused by his betrayal, rejection and the loss that I'd experienced. I obsessed and deliberated all of my options related to a future without him. I began to contemplate suicide as the only feasible one. I mean, I really thought about it. All the time… For the first time in my life, I did not want to live….

I was in shock. Numb. Paralyzed. Like one of those petrified, frozen-like trees. I couldn't move. I couldn't breathe, most of the time. I felt shame and embarrassment for not being enough of a woman to *keep* my husband. I felt an overwhelming sense of fear and panic when faced with the idea of being alone. How could he do this? To me? How could I manage things by myself? In my mind, I was a statistic: a newly divorced woman in her 40's, and a single parent with a Baby Daddy and child support issues. I didn't want to be any of that. I did not want to live as that woman and I did not want use drugs to relieve the pain and reality that I was her. Against my will…. By that time, I had been conditioned, by recovery people and my evolving program, to do everything in my power to avoid going back to the horrors of addiction. I did not want to go back to being that version of me. I didn't want that life and I didn't want this one either. I felt like I was out of options. I was at the crossroads and I had to figure out what to do….

I thought back on all the times that I had judged and been very insensitive and opinionated about women whose husbands or boyfriends had left them --- for other women. Now, I thought about my insensitivity, the callous, cold-hearted way I had handled their pain. I recalled how unsympathetic I had been about their situations. I felt so ashamed about my circumstance and the lack of empathy I'd displayed. I prayed no one would mishandle me like that. So, because of all of that, I didn't tell anyone the truth about what was happening to me for a long time. I kept my feelings, my fears, my apprehension and my pain to myself.

Kept it all a secret and suffered deeply in silence. I masked all the feelings. I couldn't face the humiliation of having lost my marriage because I refused to live with his infidelity. I thought others would judge me as harshly as I had judged. I kept the undisclosed thoughts of suicide to myself because they made me feel weak, defeated and ashamed. I felt inadequate and inferior to every woman, especially the young ones. At the age of 40, I felt old, undesirable, unattractive, unlovable and undeserving of another chance. I thought I'd never find anyone who would want to love me as I was. I felt empty and angry and hopeless, and I wanted those feelings to go away. I thought *not living* was the only remedy to ease the pain….

But, I am so grateful. I am grateful that I lived through that time and those feelings. I'm grateful I didn't follow the unending destructive thoughts that told me to end my pain with death. I am grateful that I was in recovery, surrounded by people in recovery, when the death of my marriage occurred. My friends understood my pain. They allowed me to go through the feelings and the pain without judgment. They taught me how to move through the feelings and the pain using the principles of recovery. I'm grateful because my recovery family knew how to reassure and encourage me. They cared for and nurtured me back to sanity. They loved me back to life. Seriously…. It was their unconditional love and genuine concern that inspired me and made me want to live again. I began to participate in my own recovery, and there were people there who knew what to do to help me to save me from myself. I am grateful because I am alive to tell my truth now….

What Happened Next Was...

What do you do when you've been living what you believe to be your dream and it's abruptly taken from you, despite your best efforts to hold on to it? What do you do after you go through the shame, guilt, fear, embarrassment, disappointment, anger and brutal attacks (of your own making) to your self-esteem? Just what do you do when thoughts of suicide, homicide, rage, distrust of others, feelings of isolation, loneliness, and a flood of other emotions plague you relentlessly? What do you do? Well, you do the only thing you can do to move on and live: you cry, scream, curse, and pray; you let folks comfort you, remind you that you're going to be alright. Then, you throw back the covers, you get out of bed, open the curtains and let some light shine in; you pull yourself together the best way you can, you find faith that things will get better, try to trust the process, you put one foot firmly in front of the other, and you just start walking like you're going somewhere... You just keep moving forward like you mean it. And at some point, you will. And Life will begin to make sense again. It did for me. But before it did...

I was angry. I mean, really angry. I was angry at every man that I saw on the street. I was especially mad at every middle-aged man that I saw with a younger woman. (Oh, did I mention that she was a thin little 12-year old? Okay, maybe a little older than 12, but you get my drift). Sorry, I easily digress… And any time I saw that, it reminded me of the terrible turn that my life had taken. It reminded me of his betrayal and her larceny. And that made me want to scream and yell and spit, and hit something. I wanted to destroy him and her, and anyone who reminded me of him and her. I talked crazy and reckless to folks. I cried all the time. I cursed and wanted to fight all the time. I felt like I'd been cheated, by life, all the time. I wanted to do something that would make me feel like I'd gotten back at them for what they had done to me. It reminded me of when I was a young girl in the schoolyard and someone hit or pushed me, and I didn't get to get them back. Or like when I was cheated in a game, and I wanted to get back at the cheaters for cheating, and I couldn't. It is really amazing how easily we can revert back to the old, familiar thoughts that lay dormant, buried beneath the level of consciousness. You know, all those childhood thoughts, ideas, and feelings that never really go away….

I realize that the childhood me, the little girl that remains inside of me, is still hurt from some hurts from many years ago. There was pain and scars and emotional injuries that she'd never been given the means through which she could heal. And that little girl cries out very loudly in those circumstances that re-hurt or remind her of those original hurts. The chunky little girl who was ridiculed in school still lives – in me. I have learned through the recovery process that I have to do some very intentional things to heal, not only the grown up me, but that little girl part of me, as well. I have to tend to the hurts, disappointments, unaddressed feelings, and deep-rooted trauma of the little girl inside.

I have to address the part of me that needs to get love, attention, nurturing and healing. I have to pay very close attention to those feelings, fears and hurts as they emerge. I have to ensure that when I hear her cries and screams from the recurring pain, I must do nurturing, loving things to soothe and care for her. I cannot act like *she* is not there. She is real. She is the part of me that can overtake me if the pain gets great enough. So, I take the action necessary to help my little girl to get over her issues because those issues are relevant to me. They are as relevant, if not more, as the grown woman issues that require my attention. I cannot ignore either one of those very important parts of me. One of the goals of recovery, I've found, is to reconcile the underdeveloped little girl and the unevolved grown woman into one whole, fully developed, healthy being. And that takes time and attention. It takes work. Real work….

During that time of healing and growth, I experienced some other revelations that made me re-assess, re-evaluate and make more adjustments. I had to make the decision to finally divorce my husband. I mean, he had done me wrong, but I still loved him. After all, he was my first mature love. It is not an easy task to neutralize feelings that have existed as part of your life, part of you, for decades. It is an unreasonable expectation for anyone to think that love can be turned off like water from a spigot. It cannot. Feelings are complicated and complex. Feelings move with their own rhythm, and move to their own beat and time. I had to take certain steps to become willing to let go. I had to make a real effort to release myself from him – his love, the marriage, our plans, our life. I had to accept the reality that he had left me and that he was with someone else. I had to pray for the willingness to release myself from the deep soul-ties and the eternal covenant that I had with him. I had to break my own heart. I had to do a number of practical and spiritual things, in order to move on from that relationship. I had to ask God to intervene and release me – spiritually, mentally and emotionally – from that contract. And then, it was time to file for divorce….

I remember going to the courts to get the divorce package, and crying on the train, silently sobbing in the vestibule, praying for the courage to actually execute the plan to pick up the papers. After getting them, I remember sitting on a bench outside the court, distraught about the impending death of my marriage. I cried and cried, then decided to call some recovery friends who were on call, ready to help me to get through the traumatic experience. It took me a year from that day to actually open the package and read the papers. It was such a very emotional time. So many pages, so many words, so much to read, all about what I needed to do to dissolve the marriage. It was disturbing to write down what had happened to us on paper. To write "Abandonment", in reference to what had happened, on every document, was so painful…. I knew, though, that I couldn't move forward into my future if I wasn't willing to let go of my past. So, I completed the package. I wrote every word, filled in every line through tears and gut-wrenching emotional pain. I notarized every document, paid all of the administrative fees. I personally submitted the paperwork to the court on my own. And once all the papers were processed and served, things moved pretty quickly. There was a mixed feeling of grief and relief that set in. I walked through it though, successfully, with the help of God, my family and my friends. And with every step that I took, I was miraculously strengthened, empowered, inspired. It was my way of taking control of my life again. I didn't know how significant it would be for me to make those hard decisions by myself, for myself. I didn't know that the entire process was essential to my spiritual growth and a new level of maturity. I granted me the freedom to choose. And I chose. And I began to heal. Those choices opened my mind up to the idea that the freedom to choose --- in every area --- was a right. And out of that revelation, I began to believe that maybe, just maybe, I might have the chance to love again….

Yes, the angry girl-woman met a man. A really good man who reminded her of all of her good…. And that good man liked her and began to love her, and helped her to remember that she was worth loving and that life was worth living. She and he grew up together, matured in some of their broken places, and gained an extraordinary amount of strength from each other. They both gained their smiles and laughter back. They both found a place with each other where they could live and love and trust and feel safe again. That man loved her into a place where she could stand on her own, live independently, think for herself, and aspire to be whatever she desired. He kept her from death, taught her about life, and showed her how a man and woman are supposed to love and be – together. He loved her through a significant part of her life, and stayed with her until it was time for him to go. And when I say go, I don't mean it in a negative way. I mean, he stayed with her until the God of her understanding let her know that they were both whole enough and ready to move on to the next parts of their lives.

We both needed each other to grow and to feel safe and know that we were worthy, capable and valued. We both needed time to feel appreciated and loved. We both needed time to heal from our pasts in a safe place. And though I thought the story would end differently than it did, I had learned to trust God and the process and myself. So when it ended, where there had been an empty space in my soul before he came, I had been filled up with love and care and kindness, confidence, esteem, aspiration, faith and trust in myself, and the wherewithal to be more – on my own. That man will always be a part of my story and will always have a place in my heart. I will always love him!

I had begun to heal and was able to survive my ex-husband's visits with our son. I lived through the trying times, adjusting my expectations and establishing boundaries. I needed things to be done in a way that showed respect to me and honored our son's feelings. I never expected that words like "custody" and "visitation" and "child support" would be a part of my normal conversations. Never…. I had to go to therapy about that part. In fact, it was the work that that woman did with me that made me recognize the value of the work of a Therapist. She helped me to work through some things that I didn't even know were existing issues for me. I left that experience wanting to gain the skills to help others like she'd helped me. I eventually went to school to become a Social Worker, so I could do *the work* with others. That was an unexpected product of a very dark time…

It was an intense transition, going from an intact family unit to this newly forming arrangement. I was deep in the process of recovery by then, and felt it was essential to pay very close and careful attention to details. I had to be meticulous and mindful, responsible and attentive to my son's needs. I was constantly reminded, cognizant of how the reality of his father's absence from the home affected him. I did everything in my power to not criticize or ridicule or diminish the significance of his father's role and position. At least, not in front of him. I was mindful to not talk about his father through my anger. I had to remember to not have inappropriate conversations about the father with my son, and to never make my son feel like he had to choose. I recognized that it was my husband and I who were divorcing, and that my son should never feel like he being divorced, too. I, in time, learned to accept that people have the right to choose, to make choices, and that I would not always be the choice they made. I learned a lot about powerlessness, acceptance, faith, trust, patience, tolerance, humility, and forgiveness during that time in my life.

I lived through my ex-husband remarrying that random chick. I am a survivor of that! That was a critical time that required a lot of personal work to be done. I did extensive work and experienced a considerable amount of growth. Uh huh. But, at first, I wanted to punch that woman in the face every time I saw her. Yup! Thief.... But, I was repeatedly reminded that people cannot be stolen. If they go, they go willingly. I had to remember that this was not a school yard game being played, where she was the winner, while I was the loser. I had to accept that he had chosen her, and if I failed to accept that fact, it was going to cause me to be the angry, bitter, unhinged, psycho-dramatic ex-wife. That was something that I didn't want – didn't want to be that and certainly didn't want to be that in the eyes of my son. So, I survived the reality of him and her. I worked to survive the loss of my extended family in the divorce, even though they continually reassured me that I would always belong to The Family. I went through an exorbitant amount of uncomfortability while attending every family event. I could have just stopped going, but I wouldn't. I didn't want to give him the idea that I was beaten. I didn't want her to have the satisfaction that I had conceded to her "game win". So, I suffered through that kind of pain for years. It was painful being the ex-wife, watching him from the side, living his new life with a new wife. It was even more painful seeing her pregnant with their daughter. I had to survive knowing that he'd had a daughter with someone else, and not with me. Whoa! More therapy…. I was oddly relieved when he announced his divorce from her, but had to find new strength to survive his marriage to the next bad choice. I watched him make some of the same old mistakes, and was not surprised at some of the brand new ones he'd made. I had to refrain from giving advice or suggestions about his life and his decisions. It was difficult. I had to continuously combat my distorted thinking and keep everything in its proper perspective. I had to repeatedly remind myself that that man was no longer my husband. He was no longer my responsibility, and I was no longer his. As both our lives began to unfold, I began to disentangle my life from his. I realized that I really could live a life on my own. And things got increasingly better for me once I learned to keep the focus on myself. I was slowly learning to mind my own business….

I came to know that it is possible to survive your emotions. It is also possible to survive the notion to go back to old, outdated, useless behaviors – again. I learned to resist the urges to travel down the road leading to "What-if" town – a fake place in my head that adds no value to a healthy emotional state. I use the spiritual principles of acceptance and surrender to survive the thoughts and feelings that come. You know, the feelings about life and how it was supposed to be, the maybe ifs, if only's, and all of the "If I coulda, woulda, shouldas". I have to remember to tell myself, "It is what it is!!" I began to understand, in these moments, that acceptance is the key….

I lived through the death of my brother, Billy, who passed away on my 2nd anniversary of clean time. He was one of the main people who helped to save me during active addiction. I mean, he really tried to save his little sister until he realized that he couldn't. It was the grace of God that saved me from all dangers seen and unseen during my active addiction. But often, God would use my brother to come find, fetch and rescue me from the streets. He would bring me home to my mother, and they'd both hope and pray to God that this last time would be the last time. After he died, the thought of using again and not having my big brother to come save me was a scary, but healthy fear. So, instead of changing my clean date so I wouldn't have to be sad each year on my clean date / his death date, I was reminded that I could change my thoughts and my perspective about it. That year, I decided I would stay clean in honor of my brother. And now, each year on my clean date anniversary, I celebrate his life and mine by having stayed clean for another year…..

I also lived through the experience of the death of my mother. I barely survived that! All I could tap into was my gratitude that she had had the opportunity to see me get clean, stay clean, learn to live clean, and become grounded in this new way of life. My mother had had a disproportionate amount of experience with the ugly side of addiction. She saw it all. She lived through all of things that I lived through. She saw all the rises and falls throughout the years. Just knowing what she saw still brings me indescribable pain and guilt and shame. She did not deserve to go through any of that. But, I am grateful that she was here to be a part of my recovery process for 12 years. I was able to make amends to her for 12 years. My mother was my champion, rooting and cheering me on through every failure and every success. She stood by my side, helped me to endure the loss of my husband, to persevere through the divorce, and to successfully navigate every situation and circumstance that happened before she transitioned. I am thankful that my mother lived to see me live again. She saw me go through and get through quite a few life storms. She saw me find love again – I know that gratified her. She was present to see me accomplish some remarkable things. I am so grateful that my mother lived to see me survive all of it, and that I got to live a very successful and productive life, with my Mom looking on proudly, watching her Baby go…. She lived to see me walk across the stage – for both graduate degrees – and was able to experience the successes that were born out of that. I am so grateful that she was here to see me grow long enough and strong enough to pull myself together and become a trustworthy, responsible woman. My greatest joy was that I got to be a success and saw what that looked like in her eyes. She saw me becoming the person she had always wanted me to be. I am grateful that she died knowing that I would be alright. I am so glad that I was so deep into recovery when she passed away, that the thought of using was not what I thought about. I'm grateful that I gained enough confidence in my recovery and developed enough trust in the process to believe that I did not have to use to escape the pain of her death. I know that she knew that she could leave here peacefully, and that I would not use because she had to go. I am grateful that she knew that I would be okay! I survived knowing that she did…

I have used recovery principles as the groundwork for raising my son. He is 34 years old now. He is such a good man. He's a Mama and Grandma's Boy, spoiled from all the giving that we gave to compensate for his pains and losses. We tried to give him everything so he would not feel like he'd lost out, like he'd been deprived because his father was no longer in our home. And even though there is still residue of that loss that could not be erased by any amount of stuff that we could give him, he survived too. We did spoil him. I spoil him still. But despite that, he is good and loving, caring, and genuinely loves people with his whole heart. I am so proud of who he is becoming. I used my trust in the Higher Power that I learned to rely on, to teach and raise and grow my son. I am grateful for the men in recovery (and the men in other areas of my community) who helped me to raise him. I trusted that God would fill in all of the spaces and the broken places where I could not. I came to believe that if I turned my will and my life, and all of my life concerns (which include my son), over to God's care, that He would take care of them all. And He did.…

I learned to practice patience and tolerance in my home with my son. I learned to treat him with unconditional love and respect, with compassion and empathy. I learned to listen to him – to hear his cries, to pay attention to his concerns, and to address them intentionally and purposefully. I am learning to practice acceptance of the decisions that he makes for his life, especially now that he is a man and makes grown-man decisions – without me. He has the right to make decisions concerning his life and his concerns. I am powerless over the decisions of a grown man. I am responsible to give him good orderly direction, and give him the space to grow and to choose for himself. And I cannot force him to use my guidance or reprimand him when he doesn't. I am still learning how to do this consistently. I use the principles of recovery to monitor myself when it comes to him, especially when he uses his charming, overly convincing ways to manipulate me for his own interests. After all, he is the son of two addicts, so he inherently knows how to "work the room" to get what he needs. I have learned that I do not have to succumb to the feelings of guilt and shame that come to remind me that I abandoned this child over and over when the drugs had control of my life. I am learning to forgive myself for the things that I did and for those that I didn't do pertaining to my son….

I am grateful that I had the recovery blueprint to guide me in growing a man-child successfully into adulthood. And pleased that he was influenced, conditioned by a solid foundation from The Church, a solid relationship with God, and a well-grounded recovery program. He is equipped and skillful at utilizing all of the spiritual principles in his life. He loves God, people, service, and is mindful to keep an eye on his thinking, attitudes, feelings and behaviors. The Twelve Step recovery process gave me what I needed: discipline to manage my life. I took the opportunity to impart that same discipline in the direction given to my son. I learned to let go of the past, the guilt, shame and remorse, and replaced it with patience, gratitude, integrity, love and respect. I grew into a mother, a friend and a confidant to my son. Yes, I am his friend. But, I learned that I must be his mother first….

God's grace ensured that my son would survive the sins of his mother and father. And after all that happened, my son is an ordained Pastor, a minister of music, works in law enforcement, and is studying Psychology, with a plan to help people using all of those gifts and talents. He is a good man with a good heart. He had found and married a good woman who genuinely loved him. They were married for 5 years until she passed away from a chronic illness. He was widowed by age 28. He was devastated by that loss and it really shook his faith and made him question everything. It was his faith and an unending love of God that helped him to survive that loss. A few years ago, he was blessed to have a child. And though the relationship with the child's mother did not end up as planned, he was blessed with a beautiful daughter who looks and acts just like him. It has been challenging for him (for all of us) to navigate all of the feelings, his choices, the reality of life as it is, and the turmoil that sometimes serves as a backdrop to his situation. I really wish I could fix what is broken. I wish I could help them to embrace what I've learned about loss, grief, anger, fear, disappointments, change, relationships, surrender and acceptance. I know it would help them because of how it helped me. I pray that we can all work to prevent any added collateral harm concerning the parenting and well-being of the child. They are all still finding their way in this life. And so am I….

Through that situation, I learned so much about the practical application of faith, trust, acceptance, surrender, the power of prayer, the grace of God, powerlessness, ego and pride, reactions vs. responses, and the power gained by integrating a recovery program into my life. I am grateful that I learned to be still and trust God, when I'm just not sure what do….

I am the youngest of three children. I am The Baby. I took my sister's place when I was born…. I came into the family when my parents were older, a little slower to punish, and a bit more able and apt to buy whatever they could to satisfy my needs. And quiet my noise…. My siblings were much older than me. In fact, people thought that my sister was my real mother, which really caused her great angst in my early years. My mother made her take me with her wherever she went – all the time. I became a great source of frustration to her. I was the kid sister who always wanted to be around her, follow her, hang out with her and her friends, and spend time with her and her (our) boyfriends. I was the pain-in-the-butt, nosey, chatty little sister who wouldn't get away from her. I thought she was beautiful and cool and classy, and I wanted to be her friend. That's not the way she perceived our relationship. She seemed angry with me all the time.

As I got older, I began to sense there was a bit of envy and jealousy, and a great deal of resentment about the way that I was being treated. She resented the way my parents were so lenient and indulgent with me; was insulted by what they allowed me to do and say, offended that I could cross certain lines that were forbidden for her and my brother to cross. My parents were able to provide so many more opportunities, to get things for me that were not within reach for my siblings during our parents' leaner years. When I reached young adulthood, there emerged an unspoken rivalry that subtly existed between us that no one ever spoke of. The big sister – little sister rivalry dynamic permeated every area of our relationship. My mother's unconditional love and unreasonable defense of any of my behaviors, especially during my active addiction, translated badly for my sister. Both of us were vying for the attention and approval of our mother in our own ways. Many of those feelings lingered and grew more intensely as we grew into adulthood. The antagonism and conflicts really impacted the way we acted, especially around our Mom. I think we just didn't like each other anymore…..

It wasn't until the death of my mother that my sister and I began to reach out to each other for care, concern, support, empathy, love, strength and understanding. My mother's death eradicated that rival dynamic that had existed for so long between us. It leveled the playing field. Mommy's death, that profound sense of loss, changed us almost instantly. Our need for rivalry, competition and unnecessary opposition died when she died. We became two women, equals, who were mourning the sudden loss of their mother. And since her death, we try to talk to each other regularly, almost daily, as equals, as women, sisters making the effort to re-establish trust and build a healthy relationship. We talked endlessly, and in those discussions, we began to sort through years of misunderstandings, mistaken assumptions, unverified claims, baseless conclusions, faulty perceptions, unresolved conflicts, and plain old bad information that caused some of the ongoing uneasiness between us.

I attribute the immeasurable change in us and in our relationship to our honesty (and self-honesty) and love for each other, and the inclusion of spiritual principles that ground our respective beliefs. And that really helped me with my ability to see her for who she is, and for her to see me as I am. It changed her and my capacity to value each other's opinions and perspectives, and gave us a mutual understanding of how God was working in each our lives. It is such a pleasurable experience to develop a real sisterly bond, and to see it growing into a relationship based on mutual respect and genuine gratitude for our new connection. I am grateful that we developed so many facets of our relationship, and are in each others' lives in the way that we are now. I am proud of who we have each become. Mommy would be so proud that we finally stopped the nonsense and gave up the ongoing struggle for power ….

How The Transformation Began...

DISCLAIMER

I have taken the leisure and creative license to use text that is generic – I will not violate the Traditions of *my* 12-Step program by using program language verbatim. I have also modified the language of the steps to emphasize the recovery principles for use by any reader. Though most 12-Step programs use "we" throughout their specific literature, to remind members that we go through the process using the concept of mutual support, I modified it so you can personalize the concepts and incorporate them into your self-talk, into your thinking, into various areas of your life. And by using these simple guidelines and principles, you, my friends, will find yourselves moving forward in your individual processes of recovery.

It was hearing the Twelve Steps, words, concepts repeated at every meeting I attended, that I began to make sense out of the chaos in my head. I learned to apply the underlying spiritual principles to the places within where addiction had damaged me. I used all of the steps and associated principles to change my attitudes, ideas, my thought processes and my perspective. I worked to address the things that hindered, obstacles, barriers that continuously got in the way of my plan to be and do better. *"These are the principles that make recovery possible..."*

The Twelve Steps Of Recovery

1. I admitted that I was powerless over ___ (addiction, drugs, alcohol, cigarettes, gambling, food, sexual behavior, stealing, lying, low self-esteem, situations, conditions and circumstances), that my life had become unmanageable.
2. I came to believe that a Power greater than myself could restore me to sanity.
3. I made a decision to turn my will and my life over to the care of the God as I understood Him.
4. I made a searching and fearless moral inventory of myself.
5. I admitted to God, to myself and to another human being the exact nature of my wrongs.
6. I became entirely ready to have God remove all these defects of character.
7. I humbly asked God to remove my shortcomings.
8. I made a list of all persons I had harmed, and became willing to make amends to them all.
9. I made direct amends to such people wherever possible, except when to do so would injure them or others.
10. I continued to take personal inventory, and when I was wrong promptly admitted it.

11. I sought through prayer and meditation, to improve my conscious contact with God as I understood Him, praying only for knowledge of His will for me and the power to carry that out.
12. Having had a spiritual awakening as a result of these steps, I tried to carry this message to others and to practice these principles in all of my affairs.

It was the spiritual principles, recovery concepts and the idea of a recovery process that opened my mind to the possibility that change could happen for me. The recovery process allowed me to recognize opportunities to do something different when presented, and has shown me how to change things about me, change my thinking, perception and perspective, and achieve a better quality of life. My living today was made possible only by continued application of these principles in all life situations, by the people in recovery who supported and guided me, and God's Grace that continually kept my head, heart and spirit in the right place. It's what happened in my lived experience that transformed me into the woman that I am.

So, just how will this recovery stuff work for me, you ask? Well, after I'd learned to pay attention to myself, I began to notice the inappropriate thinking that continued to creep into my consciousness and the bad behaviors that resulted from it. After becoming honest with myself about who and how I really was, and considering the idea that maybe there was something unbalanced going on, I became open to the idea that maybe I really could use new approaches to tackle and manage life and its presenting situations. I began to see that I needed to replace some of the old ideas and to discover some new ones. I was told that I might need to recondition my thinking; that maybe it was time to obtain and incorporate new information into my current thought process. I was also told that I should refrain from denying and resisting the truth, and embrace the idea that my thinking had been severely affected, biased and burdened with old mess that needed to be treated and cleansed. A brain-washing, of sorts...

I learned how to integrate the principles into my thinking, using the steps as my guidelines. And once I learned to do that, it was essential that I began to address and change some other things.

How Spiritual Principles Transformed Me

STEP ONE

I admitted that I was powerless over ________ (addiction, drugs, alcohol, cigarettes, gambling, food, sexual behavior, stealing, lying, low self-esteem, situations, conditions and circumstances), that my life had become unmanageable.

Principles: honesty, open-mindedness, willingness, humility, acceptance

How It Works for Me:

It is important for me to stay in tune with my thoughts, feelings, ideas and anything that affects my thinking. It is also important to stay in touch with reality. It is just as important to recognize when it's necessary for me to surrender to the reality of things. I cannot control people, places, things, situations, circumstances, or conditions. I have to see and accept what is happening when it is happening. I have no power over the things that happen, but I do have the ability to make a decision about my response to them. I have developed the ability to accept reality as it is, to surrender to the fact that a particular reality exists, and to choose my response to that reality. I am powerless over what and how life presents, but I am not powerless over my behaviors. I do not have to drink, get high, eat, shop, have sex, fight or do anything else that I used to do to get through the feelings or situations. I do not have to act out. I do not!! That's the old way of handling feelings. I have a choice. I can think it out. Talk it out. Pray it out. Cry it out. Write it out. Or wait it out.… I can stop myself before I do something that will cause regret later. I have learned to be open-minded to others' opinions or information that is given to me. I have the choice and the free will to hear it, despite what I may think or how I feel. I have learned that there might just be another way, other than my way, and that I should be willing to, at least, consider it. I have learned to accept the truth as it is, and am willing to see things as they really are. I told you that I had become very comfortable using denial (what's happening is not happening) and fantasy (my imagined version of what's happening). Both of those points in consciousness, neither of which are centered in reality, have always created the opening for me to detach from the truth about my reality. And if I go to the old approaches of dealing with things, I will drink / drug / smoke / eat / sex / shop / fight my way out of the feeling and into another feeling that's not based in the truth. Then, the results of acting out on my feelings will come. And this is where the unmanageability seeps in. So, instead of using or running (in my head) to an imaginary place, I have become very skilled at choosing and changing what I do. I can choose a healthy response to any situation. Sometimes, I can do that on my own. Sometimes, I need help from the people in my life. And sometimes, I go to God and ask for His help and guidance. I have found that The Serenity Prayer is always a powerful tool that helps to bring me back into the moment of my present reality: *"God, grant me the serenity to accept the things I cannot change, the courage to change the things that I can, and the wisdom to know the difference."* What a wonderful thing it is to know that I do not have to act out or respond in the same old ways that I've always responded. Wonderful…

In this process, humility has allowed me to accept my own human-ness (capacity and limits), to know when it's time to surrender, and to recognize when I have done all that I could. If I were a powerful fighter, and I got into the ring with a fighter more powerful than me, I would have to know when it's time to surrender and stop the fight. I know that I would be beaten if I did not. My experience has proven that. Life, reality, is a powerful opponent and I cannot always win. I have learned to surrender to it. And surrender doesn't make me weak. It makes me smart and skillful, and affords me the opportunity to live and fight again.

Step One means that I do not have control over people, places, things, situations, circumstances or other things that present themselves. This step reminds me that I shouldn't try to control because trying to control does not work. I cannot win using the same old approaches. I will lose again and again…. Trying to control produces unmanageability in my life – both inner and outer unmanageability. I have learned many different ways to manage things that overwhelm and come seemingly to defeat me. There are always lessons to be learned from the challenges of life. I can accept. I can surrender. I can move on if I have the right perspective.

Step One reminds me that there is room for me to re-envision a situation and change my perspective about its reality in relation to me. I can get through anything, if I am honest, open-minded, willing, and accepting of the truth. And when my human ability is not enough to get me through, I must acknowledge that I need help from something greater than me. I am responsible to recognize when I am in that place, and to know where to get the help that I need....

STEP TWO

I came to believe that a Power greater than myself could restore me to sanity.

Principles: open-mindedness, willingness, faith, trust, humility

How It Works for Me:

It took leap of of faith and a shift in my overall thought process to believe that if I needed help, it was okay to ask for it. It was long into the recovery process before I even considered how flawed and slightly askew my thinking was. At some point, I began to see that if the program people kept saying I needed to be restored to sanity, there was a possibility that I may have been thinking/acting/behaving in ways that were unreasonable, impractical, and maybe just a little insane. It took some time for me to get honest about things that I had done during active addiction. It was even more challenging to admit some of the insanity that I had practiced after coming into recovery. I would have preferred a word other than *insanity* to describe my behavior, but when I looked honestly at some of my ways, there was really little uncertainty about the insanity. I did do the same things over and over, while expecting different results. So…

In the beginning of my recovery, I had a different concept of what a "power greater than myself" was. They explained that there were different types of powers greater than me that could help to restore me to soundness and stability. They told me to attend meetings (power) because meetings were where the basis, the source of recovery happened. The 'starting to believe' process led me to talk to other recovery people to hear their experiences and perspectives. The people were a power greater than me. I began to read the books and pamphlets, and listened to recorded materials (power). That helped me to understand addiction, how it affected me, and how recovery could help me. I went to meetings regularly and that's where I got more information, more hope, more evidence that recovery really worked. I gained a sense of camaraderie with a group of people just like me. It took courage to get and use a sponsor, a guide (power) to support me. I had to push my ego and pride aside, and eventually, asked someone to help me understand the process and the program.

I starting listening to others share about prayer and the power of prayer and how it supported their recovery process. I began to pray. At that time, I was praying more for something than to something, as I was still dealing with the idea of who and what my ultimate Higher Power was. My thinking initially went to fear and I had an unwillingness to even deal with God. The God that I knew was an angry, wrathful, unforgiving God, and I could not go to Him to help me. It took some time to work through the guilt, shame, remorse, and the feelings of being unfaithful to the moral teachings I'd learned about the God of my younger days. I wrestled with the idea that my Higher Power could be whatever and how ever I defined it. Eventually, with an opened mind, I put my faith in other recovering people because I saw how these new ideas were working for them. I came to trust the process. Humility required that I stop struggling with the thought that I could rely only on my own thinking. I needed to let others in. I needed their help. I needed to ask for it. I needed to let them teach and guide me. I came to believe that I could trust them to do that. I listened as others expounded on the journey that led them to believe. I had listened to their stories about an evolving relationship with a Higher Power and I wanted that, too. They said I only had to be willing to believe that there was a power available, a power that would able to help keep me clean and sane. I began to believe that I could be restored to a soundness of mind and a normal way of living, if I just trusted and followed their way. I trusted the people, the program and the process. I learned to use these sources of power to help myself do something different, especially when I was angry, frustrated, sad, lonely, or felt feelings that I couldn't identify. During this part of the process, I began to re-evaluate my belief system: my core values, morals, beliefs, views and life philosophy. I started to redefine my standards, by aligning my belief system with the principles of the program. I began to expand my concept of a power-filled being, a limitless power, a trustworthy Higher Power that I could rely on. I was slowly being introduced to the God that I have come to know….

STEP THREE

I made a decision to turn my will and my life over to the care of the God as I understood Him.

Principles: surrender, willingness, faith, trust, commitment

How It Works for Me:

In developing my understanding of God, I was led to look to the evidence in my life to re-establish what and who I believed God really was. I realized that it was my choice to decide if the God of my understanding was to be the angry punishing God of my childhood, who expected me to pay for my past indiscretions. Or if He was to be a loving, caring forgiving God who had only plans for my best future in mind. This decision-making part of the process helped to reaffirm my freedom of choice to believe what and how I wanted to believe. The evidence showed that the God who had expended grace and mercy on my behalf, had to have been loving, caring, and forgiving to allow me to survive what I had survived. God had not only spared me, He'd given me a chance to start over and create an amazing life for myself. When I began to think like this, I struggled less, and in time, I surrendered. I had begun to believe that God really loved me, really cared for all that concerned me, and wanted a better, more prosperous and productive life for me. He had a purpose and a plan for me. The undeniable evidence in my life, as it was developing, proved that to me. I gradually made the decision to turn my will (ideas, thinking, feelings, emotions) and my life (everything else: health, family, friends, relationships, home, jobs, future plans, etc.) over to His care. I accepted that

God could do a much better job of caring for me than I'd been able to do for myself. This all meant that I could decide, consciously, intentionally decide to relinquish my self-centered, obsessively focused, self-absorbed will over to God. I trusted that it would be okay, and that I would be okay in His care. That decision allowed me to become more successful and effective in most areas of my life. I try to live a God-reliant life, which means, I depend on God. I make a conscious effort to do that. I talk to God regularly, formally and in casual conversations. I ask for His help consistently, request His guidance in every area of my life, and try to remain aware of how He expects someone in His care to behave. I work hard to be aware of other people, of their feelings and needs, and try to avoid offending or harming them. I know when I need to check myself, to turn over my attitude, mood or thoughts; when I need to turn over my plans; when I need to turn over my family issues, financial concerns, health status, potential distresses, and ongoing cares to Him. And you know what is the best part about the turning it over process? When I turn things over, I no longer have to carry the weight, and manage the burden of making things happen. I no longer have to be in control. I understand that God is in control. I accept that God is in control. I practice letting go and letting God be in control. And in those times when I fail to remember who's in charge, He reminds me. And those reminders are often painful signs that I need to relinquish my thoughts of control or suffer the consequences….

I don't want to infer that I live as a mindless, mechanical robot. I mean, I know that I no longer have to control or manipulate the world, and all the people in it, to get what I need. I can give it my best effort and do what I can, and trust that God will make the outcomes happen as He has designed. He gives me what I need based on His plans for me. I have learned to trust God with everything. And I find that the more I trust Him, the more He shows that He is faithful to deliver, and my level of trust in Him grows even more from that. I trust God with me and all that concerns my life. I have a strong faith that He will work things out for me. I have come to believe that in this process, and I've committed to share these lessons with whomever will listen. It gives me a great sense of comfort in knowing that all things are working together for my good and that I am in God's care. I am in his amazing care....

STEP FOUR

I made a searching and fearless moral inventory of myself.

Principles: willingness, honesty, courage, faith, trust

How It Works for Me:

Well.... It took some time for me to look at myself honestly. I tell you, denial will keep you believing that you are something that you are not. Denial will allow you to tell yourself lies that you know are untrue, long enough for you to begin believe them yourself. The 4th Step was the method through which I took my first honest look at myself --- EVER!! It took a couple of times before I was really able to get really honest with myself. I could only look at surface issues in the beginning. But as time progressed and the need for a more in-depth examination of self became clear, I had to peel the onion some more. I had to go deeper and look at the issues that were hindering me from being my best. It took a tremendous amount of courage to begin the process, and it took a deeper level of commitment to persevere despite the fear of what I would find. It was during the divorce that I really began to take a deeper look because my life (and my emotional stability) depended on it. By the time I went in deeper, I was certain that I could trust God to carry me through the self-appraisal process (After all, He had just pulled me out of the suicidal 'divorce' depression). I genuinely trusted that I would get better if I went through a thorough inventory while in His care. I moved forward in the process with the help of an experienced recovery member (my sponsor). The process forced me to look at my defects of character, as well as the assets of my personality. The process enabled me to examine the unresolved pain, to look at the source of some of my pain, to search through the conflicting messages that formed my thinking. I searched through some of the hurts that shaped my fear-based thinking. I looked at harbored resentments, anger, guilt, shame and fear, my feelings, my relationships, my secrets, other issues, and what they all meant to me. I looked at things that I thought would go with me to the grave…. It was an exhausting, challenging process that was well worth the effort. It was quite a feat to put it all out there on paper. Undeniable facts that I put on paper. That made it all real. Undeniably real! The inventory is likened to the task of a shop owner – every so often, s/he is required to examine the stock that is there on the shelves, to determine what is usable and should be kept, and what is outdated and needs to be discarded. I like that analogy. I am responsible to regularly inventory *my shop*. I am my shop. This type of personal assessment can be done by anyone who wants to clean up shop and move forward with their business. Many years later, I regularly use the 4th Step inventory process because my ability to live free and stay clear is worth the effort.

STEP FIVE

I admitted to God, to myself and to another human being the exact nature of my wrongs.

Principles: trust, courage, self-honesty, commitment

How It Works for Me:

So, this 5th step was another unnerving part of the inventory process. I didn't feel it necessary to go through all my stuff and discuss it with my sponsor again. And I was sure God was well aware of every single thing that had happened to me. But, because I wanted to experience all the benefits of the process, I felt compelled to follow the direction of my predecessors. My sponsor recommended that we look very closely at who I was, how I'd become who I was, who I was becoming, where I was in my recovery and in my life, and what I needed to do to get even better. I really had to pray a lot before I began because I needed courage to trust in my sponsor even more, a willingness to tell more of the truth, the commitment to continue on and not put the work down and leave things undone. My sponsor explained why I had to tell God (to reaffirm my 3rd Step decision; to gain humility and a sense that He cared for me despite past actions; to connect with His presence), myself (to tell me the truth, to break the patterns of denial, to accept myself unconditionally) and another human being (connection to humanity; help to see fantasy, blame, core of issues). I gained an understanding of what 'exact nature' means. It means the why of the situation. Not what I did (Step 4) - why I did what I did (Step 5). What was and is still driving me? What was I feeling when I did what I did? What are the patterns and where'd they begin? What underlies the patterns? What are the common threads? It gave me an opportunity to come face to face with myself. Not only who I thought I was, but who I actually was. Humility is the ability to see yourself clearly – to accept your human-ness and all its frailties. What makes me tick? What makes me run? What makes me act the way that I do? What underlies the parts of me that are not in full focus? What the exact nature of my behaviors, especially my wrong behaviors? I finally gained the courage to look at myself without fear. It was frightening and exciting to face me and everything about me. It was the beginning of a process of unconditional acceptance of myself through a reality-based lens. I am more able to accept my good and my bad, to recognize all of my defective parts and my positive features. I can accept myself as neither better than nor worse than the next person. I just am. I learned through this process to accept me just as I am. My sponsor accepted me just as I am. God accepts me just as I am. My commitment is to continually practice the principle of self-acceptance, and to strive for better in all the areas that need it. And that keeps me open and looking, and paying attention to all of me....

STEP SIX

I became entirely ready to have God remove all these defects of character.

Principles: commitment, perseverance, willingness, faith, trust, self-acceptance

How It Works for Me:

The 6th Step work allowed me to identify the defective areas of my character, to look closely at my patterns of behavior, and to examine how I behave – over and over again. The work that I'd done in the previous steps compelled me to be more honest with myself, and raised my awareness of the serious need for a persistent desire to change - everything. I just got really tired of my bad behaviors and was ready to change them. The previous work that I had done fueled the process of examining how my behavior affected my life in so many different ways. I had quite a few defects of character, basic traits blown out of proportion by self-centered fear and a desperate need to get whatever I wanted. These defects had to be addressed and removed, or at least minimized to a manageable state. It was here in this part of the process that I learned how and what to monitor, and how to control my desires to do what I wanted to get what I wanted. I committed to paying better attention my behavior in every situation, and made a conscious decision to do better. I wanted to want to do the right thing for the right reason. I was willing to act better and do better – for myself and with others. That took time, energy, commitment and faith that I could and would do this personal surveillance for my own good. The subtle changes over time created an increased belief that the process was effective in helping me to change me. It took trust that God would continue to be a source of power for me, and that He would help me to be better and obtain better outcomes in my life situations. I learned to stop myself – in the moment – and to think about my actions <u>before</u> I reacted to what I was thinking. Just stopped and took a moment…. I was amazed at the power of what that shift did for me. The ability to do that one thing increased my belief in myself and in my capacity to be better. Did I do it perfectly? Absolutely not! But, have I gotten better as a result? Absolutely have! I began to recreate a vision for myself; I began to redefine myself, without the old patterns getting in my way. I have gained a whole new idea of who I can be. I know that God has His Hand in everything that helps me to redesign the course for my life. I feel a sense of relief each time I see myself getting ready to do the same old things that got me the same old results. I am living proof that we each have the power, the capacity to change anything about ourselves that is defective, destructive or counterproductive to attaining goals and dreams and vision. I know that God is helping me to help myself with the things that I have the power to change. But, for those things that I know are out of my human ability to change, my next course of action is to ask God to help me. So, I do…

STEP SEVEN

I humbly asked God to remove my shortcomings.

Principles: surrender, trust, faith, patience, humility

How It Works for Me:

By the time I approached the 7th Step, I had surrendered my old idea of who I was, by rigorously dismantling my false image, ego, pride, arrogance, and the unrealistic view that I'd held of myself for so long. The preceding step had prepared me with a better perspective, the humility needed to approach God with my concerns, and the willingness to accept whatever He would do to remove or correct my imperfect ways. This humbling part of process left me open, willing, and trusting. It made me tap into my faith in order to trust that God could and would remove unnecessary parts of my character, and perform a rebuilding of my overall personality. The evidence that I'd seen in others and the proof of changes seen in my own life provided a foundation of what I needed to take my relationship with God to an even deeper level. I began to be unashamed and unapologetic about relying on something other than myself for direction and help. I was unafraid to trust in a Higher Power, something that I could not see or touch. I was humbled by the phenomenal nature of my Higher Power's power, and sincerely believed that He could remove all of my shortcomings (defective behavior in action), if I asked. I found that my part was to ask Him, with a posture of humility, and trust that He could do for me what I could not do for myself. And I learned to have patience with myself through the times when I wasn't so willing to change. I trusted that God would help me in those times, too. It was very challenging, at first, to go to the place in my spirit where humility is housed, but then, I realized that the more I went in there, the easier it was to go there. It became easier to communicate with my God from that place. And the more I talked to Him, the easier it was to ask Him for help. And each time I asked and He worked on things on my behalf. I got better and things got better too. The more He did for me, the more I trusted and believed in Him. God proved that He was trustworthy. My relationship with God helped me to seek out and begin to build a more spiritually grounded life. And as I matured spiritually, I began to desire more peace and less conflict in my physical life. I wanted peace, not only on the inside, for myself, I wanted to examine and repair any damage or harm that I'd caused others. It was time to begin to heal the harm that was done to my relationships with the people around me. I took another step of faith, trusted the process, and became willing to do the work to fix things....

STEP EIGHT

I made a list of all persons I had harmed, and became willing to make amends to them all.

Principles: honesty, courage, willingness, compassion

How It Works for Me:

At this point, I had become much more effective at getting my thinking and behavior in check. I wanted to honestly examine the damage that my behavior had caused others, and to rectify what had been broken in the fray. I had taken responsibility for my defective behavior, now it was time for me to examine the wreckage of my past and be accountable for any harm done. I would like to say that I was blameless, and that I'd only harmed myself. But, I didn't, so I couldn't… There were amends that needed to be made in order to resolve, repair and restore. It is so hard for self-centered people to look at the part they play – in anything. I would like to believe that it was perfectly okay for me to just move on with my life without addressing any of it. But, this part of the process required that I summon up the courage needed to identify any harm that I'd caused and address it. All of it! I had to examine my part. Had to process it. Own it. Develop the willingness to take responsibility for it, and be responsible to correct what I'd done to people who cared about me. The things that I had done. This was a hard task…. I had to go back through my work to look at my 4th Step (the behaviors) and 6th Step (the character defects and associated behaviors), in order to address what I'd done and how that affected and harmed others. I am not the girl who likes to confront my own issues. I don't like to be wrong --- about anything. But this process made me step outside of that familiar place, eliminate any denial about the truth of what was done, and begin to develop another level of honesty, humility and compassion. Man, oh man…! I listed everyone caught in the whirlwind of my destructive attitude and behaviors (family, friends, institutions, community). I was instructed to even put myself on the list for all the damage that I'd caused in my own life (career, health, finances, self-worth). Deep, right? Despite my fears of what was to come, I trusted in God and my sponsor, and had faith that I'd gain the strength and courage needed to take this task seriously. I looked at all of it.

As a result of this part of the recovery process, I learned the importance of owning my stuff -- my behavior, my part and how my stuff affects others. I developed empathy in this process. I learned quite a bit about honesty, courage, willingness, and forgiveness during this work. It was so new to me, and I was like a salmon swimming upstream, fighting the current with every stroke. But, I gained an understanding of the importance of this step's work for the health of my recovery. I needed to do all of this in preparation for the next work to be done….

STEP NINE

I made direct amends to such people wherever possible, except when to do so would injure them or others.

Principles: humility, love, forgiveness

How It Works for Me:

In my head, this was an impossible thing to do – to tell on myself by "copping to my mistakes". After looking at the list of damage that I'd caused, it was my obligation to make amends to those people, with the hope of receiving forgiveness. If I had not done all of the work in preparation for this step, I could not have advanced and followed through with the idea of it. But, by now, I was tired of eluding people I had harmed, in hopes of avoiding the discussion of my past behavior. I had begun to accept myself, accept my truths, take responsibility for my actions, and was willing to hold myself accountable for my wrongs and for my part. I felt like a mature, responsible adult, for the first time in my life. I felt able to stand and face every life situation, without running, hiding or feeling guilt, shame or embarrassment. It was what it was. And all I could do was be willing to make amends for my behavior and any harm I caused. I will tell you, I was fearful to face things in the beginning. But as time moved on, I got better at taking responsibility – with the help of God and my recovery friends. I learned to let go of my expectations regarding the outcomes – What would they say when I exposed the ugly truth? Would they accept my amends? Would they reject me? Would they forgive me? I had to trust fully that God would carry me through each amends-making effort, regardless of the outcomes. I learned that I could accept the outcomes once I'd had the courage to do my part. I also realized that each time I stood up to face my fears and address the truth about me, I got stronger. I got better. I really did. I took the opportunity to set things right. And at every instance, I experienced a great sense of freedom and relief. Whether the amends were accepted or not…. And though I still have some amends that have not been made because opportunity has not presented or the persons are not accessible, I am willing. And that's what counts! As a result of these exercises in genuine humility, I gained a better perspective of myself and of others – we are all just trying to live and be, and do the best we can. I have become more willing to live out loud with greater humility, acceptance, empathy, identification with the human condition, forgiveness, freedom, gratitude and unconditional love. It was in this part of the process that I began to care….

STEP TEN

I continued to take personal inventory and when I was wrong promptly admitted it.

Principles: self-discipline, honesty, integrity

How It Works for Me:

Recovery has produced an amazing transformation of this girl here. I never thought I could make any of the changes that I've made. Sometimes, I don't even recognize myself. There has been a stripping and rebuilding process in effect, as a result of the recovery work. This component of the step work begins the maintenance part of the process, which requires that I keep up the good work. Step Ten provides the opportunity for me to keep an eye on me, to continue building my awareness of my thought processes and my behaviors. I can see myself coming (from way down the block) and can stop myself quicker – because I want to. I want to be better. So, I need to be aware. I need to always be aware of my feelings, disposition, attitude, my interactions with others, my defects of character at work. I have to surveil me. I must stay on top of my unresolved issues, on my little girl, my unhealed hurts, and my quick-fire reactions. I have to pay attention when old habits reemerge, or when old ideas seem like good ideas, or when past behavior that didn't work in the past seems like a good thing to do now. The 10th Step makes me keenly aware of everything going on in and around me, and reminds that I will always need help from God (or another source of power). This step helps me to gauge my behavior and to keep it in check. I learned to discipline myself – to tell myself "no" when "no" is the appropriate answer. I have learned to deny myself the luxury of doing whatever I feel like doing when I feel like it. I practice disciplining myself. It is called self-discipline. It is what grown folks do. I have the ability to identify right from wrong, and to do the right thing because it is the right thing. And when I fail to do so (which happens more frequently than I'd like to admit), I am better able to clean up my current wreckage. I want to avoid the *waxy build-up* of new damage. I am able to admit when I am wrong. I am able to make immediate amends when I am wrong. And when needed, I am able to make amends to myself, because sometimes, I wrong myself. I'm a big girl, now. I know when I'm holding on to old ways, imposing my stuff for my self-interest. I know when I'm acting self-righteously, manipulatively, inappropriately, or in other ways that are immature for a woman of a certain age. I do know. And because I no longer like acting out with negative, useless behaviors, I've been working it out. I act better, so I don't have to admit to wrongs as often as I did in the past. A personal inventory at this stage, allows me to reflect on my actions, examine each encounter, address mistakes, identify the origin of bad behavior, adjust my perspective and perception, and decrease the chance of repeating that behavior again.

I also examine myself for good things that I've done, moments that I've done something good for someone else, been of service in some way, gone beyond my obligation despite the inconvenience. I learned to give myself some praise for doing right. That is necessary in this process, too. It is necessary to pat yourself on the back, give yourself a high-five for a job well done. And not in an egotistical, self-centered way. No, no…. In a loving, caring, *"Woman, look at how much better you've gotten! Congrats to you for your good behavior!"* way.

I have developed a sense of connectiveness to others in a way that I never experienced before. I have gained a true ideal of integrity from these new practices. I have let go of false images, of my masked identity, and of the fear of being wrong. It is okay to be wrong. It is human to be wrong sometimes. Being wrong doesn't make me inadequate or un-valuable or stupid. It just means that there is more work to be done. Each day, I try to just be. I have gained a great sense of freedom by just being. It is said that the true value is in being yourself. I am learning to just be me. And it really ain't that bad being me….

STEP ELEVEN

I sought through prayer and meditation, to improve my conscious contact with God as I understood Him, praying only for knowledge of His will for me and the power to carry that out.

Principles: commitment, humility, courage, faith

How It Works for Me:

So, here I am. Free to be myself. Comfortable in my own skin. Living and enjoying life without the fear of living or the dread of what's to come. So, what do I do now? Once I began to live fully, intentional about becoming my authentic self, I was left open to seek out purpose for my life. I began to search for the path that God had set for me, for the work that I was supposed to be doing. I was looking for *the more,* the *next steps,* God's plan for my life. My human condition was better, but my spirit yearned for more of what God could do for me and for what I could do for God. And for others…. The better I got, the more I wanted to be even better. I wanted a deeper relationship, a closer connection with God. I began to read and listen more. I began to question everything. I started infusing some of the biblical teachings I'd attained in ministerial studies long ago, to improve my understanding of God. My spirit was yearning, longing, hungry for knowledge and truth. I knew that I didn't want to get caught up in literal dogma and rituals and theory. I wanted to improve my spiritual condition, and get myself aligned and in right-standing with God's desired place for me. I needed more. I began to pray more. First, in the old traditional way that I'd been taught, but that was not sufficient for me. I needed to talk to God in a *new* way, in a way that reflected how I'd begun to understand Him. I needed to approach Him according to the evolving nature of our relationship. I began to pray in the morning and at night. Then, I found myself praying, talking to Him, whenever I needed to have a conversation with Him. Life is challenging. I needed to talk to Him about it. I began to talk to Him about my fears, troubling situations, times of joy, gratitude and appreciation; in weary, trying times, and in times that I just needed refuge, direction or comfort. I learned to talk to God – out loud – as if He were a confidante walking next to me. I also learned how to still my mind, so I could listen for His answers. My awareness that God was with me – everywhere and in everything – grew. My commitment to the process prompted me to include God in all my affairs. God knows my financial situation. He can do something about that. He is knows about my health conditions. He has a word to say about that. He knows what I need. He has

His hand in *my everything*. After all, I had made a decision in the 3rd Step part of this process, to turn things over to His care….

And as my prayer life, spiritual condition and relationship with God changed, so did the way that He revealed Himself in my life. God's Will for my life, as I understand it is for me to stay clean, be my authentic self, stay clean, be me, practice principles conscientiously, trust Him in all things, make genuine efforts to be my best, help others and be of service willingly, love others without conditions, laugh often, acknowledge the beauty that life offers, pursue dreams with hope and enthusiasm, trust my heart, and seek Him always (not necessarily in that order). I am committed to doing those things.

Additionally, I have learned how to incorporate the principles into my life, so I better align myself with His Will. God, and life as it presents, affords me countless opportunities to practice love, humility, trust, faith, hope, courage, perseverance, honesty, compassion, patience, tolerance, resilience, God-reliance, and other spiritual principles. I like what happens to me when I replace negativity with spiritual principles. I like who I become in those moments. It is through prayer and meditation that I have improved my conscious contact with God. It is through that contact that I am developing an awareness of just how great God is at putting us in our place. I am watching how He has paved a road for me to find myself and my purpose. I am moving on this journey toward service to Him and others. I have come to realize that the painful parts of my experience were not in vain. There was reason and purpose behind it all. There is a predestined plan, ordained by God, in place for each of us. My experiences are valuable and serve a higher purpose. I believe His Will for me is to use my life lessons to help others to learn theirs. I feel blessed to know that I am a part of God's incredible plan.

STEP TWELVE

Having had a spiritual awakening as a result of these steps, I tried to carry this message to others and to practice these principles in all of my affairs.

Principles: unconditional love, selflessness, steadfastness

How It Works for Me:

As this 12th Step experience unfolds in my life, I feel like I am living a whole new existence in a brand new life. I mean, it has been a long, slow process, but the changes over the years have been extraordinary and have yielded some amazing results. The recovery work has illuminated my thinking, my behavior has been refined, and my spirit is enlightened and refreshed by it all. I've had many spiritual awakenings, as a result of working these steps in my life. I am different, as a result of the step work. I am changed, as a result of the integration of spiritual principles into my daily living. My life is a by-product of a well-worked recovery program. I am inspired to continue my growth and to deepen my connection with the God who makes it all possible.

I am responsible to share the hope that change is possible. I am obligated to tell others that recovery from any life concern is achievable. I am required to encourage and help others to find a better way for themselves. It is my responsibility to share my truth – my experience, strength and hope. It is my duty to do for others what was done freely for me. It is my duty to work diligently, in any service that fulfills God's promises and plans for people. It is not only my honor, it is my privilege to be in service to God, and to be of service to others. There is a great sense of belonging that overcomes me when I think about all God had to maneuver to get me to here….

My intention is to make every effort to move my own interests out of the way, practice spiritual principles in all that I do, be selflessly committed, steadfast in my efforts, and help others to attain the promised freedom that recovery offers. Today, I allow God to use me in whatever way He needs. I am grateful that He does. This is my reasonable service for all that He has done for me….

Whatever **it** is, you can work through and change it using the principles of recovery. You can work it out!! You can Step out of it!! You can recover from anything…..

After Thought....

> Life is amazing. And then it's awful.
> And then it's amazing again. And
> in between the amazing and the awful
> its ordinary and mundane and routine.
> Breathe in the amazing, hold on through
> the awful, and relax and exhale during
> the ordinary. That's just living
> heartbreaking, soul-healing, amazing,
> awful, ordinary life. And it's
> breathtakingly beautiful."
>
> - LR Knost

I feel responsible to keep working on a mature, realistic view of myself, of others and of this world. I am grateful for the ability to get better with myself and others. I appreciate opportunities that life presents through the challenges and twists and turns. I know God allows these things as character-building experiences for me.

So, I am here today and living well – alone. I don't have a man in my life, but, I have a peace, a sense of calm and serenity, and an unyielding trust in God. I am sure that He will bring the right person into my life when the time is right – when both of us are whole, healthy beings equipped to engage with a life partner. I no longer have a controlling sense of urgency to have a man by my side to validate my existence or make me feel whole. I am a whole, complete woman. I am self-assured and confident about my worth. I know that I have immeasurable personal value. I believe that God is pleased with me. I know that He made me perfectly, a designer original with His personal touches who I am. I tell myself that I am amazing! I am a phenomenal Woman! I am enough! I am more than enough!!. I tell myself, because I should, that I am intelligent, competent, resourceful, and am more than capable of sustaining myself by my own means. I am gifted, skilled to accomplish any ambition that I conceive. I am practicing: re-evaluating my values, re-assessing my standards, constructing new life goals, setting stronger expectations for myself, and holding myself accountable to achieve them. I trust the process of change. I am learning to trust myself more, and to trust my thinking, my judgment, my intuition, and my heart. I trust the people who I've allowed into my life. I trust the things that I am doing outside of my comfort zone. I trust that Got has equipped me for everything that has and will come into my life. And I trust that the God who cares for me will protect me from any dangers that I cannot see for myself. I am prepared to move into the next level of success that He has prepared for me….

I am my own woman – finally. I live with dignity and purpose. That's a far cry from the self-conscious little girl-woman, driven by poor self-image, low self-worth, low self-esteem, lack of discipline, and the weight of others' opinions wearing me down. I, often, have to think my way into good behavior or practice behaving myself into better thinking.

Better thoughts create better actions. Sometimes, all I can do is *act as if,* until it is….

My confidence has improved by hearing myself speak according to the things I believe are God's desires, plans and will for me. My faith comes by hearing – me. I speak about things "that be not as though they were", until they actually are. I utilize self-talk regularly. I talk myself into believing the positive, and in the reality of all the possibilities. I remember to tell myself that I am worthy. I am not a mistake. I practice self-affirmation, to remind myself of the greatness that is in me. The greatness that God sees in me. I believe God was meticulous in making me just as I am. I believe He was confident to let me go through what I went through because He knew that it was all necessary, and knew that He would get me to the place I needed to be to become me as I am. He orchestrated everything perfectly, and on purpose, for my sake. Just for today, I am exactly where I need to be, exactly where I should be. That's how my recovery works for me….

I love to watch TV Ministers for encouragement and guidance. So one day, I was watching Bishop T. D. Jakes (my Pastor-in-my-head), and he was speaking about the power of thought. He talked about how God created the world with His thoughts, and how imperative it is for us to have the courage to use our own thoughts to create what we want in our lives and in our world. He talked about how the world is dumbing down when it comes to God and righteousness and faith. He said we have to have the courage to be ourselves and put our unique thoughts into creating what God made us to create. In that moment, I felt like I was on the right track with this writing thing, particularly, when he said that God had already given us everything that we need to be great, and was waiting for us to put our thoughts and our actions into living according to our greatness. So, right after Bishop Jakes' message, Joyce Meyers came on and talked about how she always used to wish that she was different – she would wonder why God had made her hips so wide, her feet so big, and her voice so deep. She used to continually complain about how God had made her. She wanted to be different than the Joyce that God had made her to be. Then, one day she had a revelation: God had made her exactly as He wanted her – God believed that everything about her was good and right. He made her exactly as He wanted her. She talked about her past wishes that her life had been different – wondered why God had allowed her to go through such horrendous experiences in her childhood, why she had had to go through what she went through with her father. During her talk, I identified with those feelings – how I'd spent so much time asking God why I was the way that I was, and why did He let me go through the horrors of addiction. But, I know, as Joyce alluded, that I would have been a much less effective, less purposeful version of myself had I not gone through what I went through, survived, learned from it, and became willing to articulate the possibility of surviving those situations with others. I am reminded, through those ministers' teachings, that God designed me according to His Will to fulfill a specific purpose. He predestined me to live in my own brand of greatness and anointed me to be of service in my own particular way. They instilled in me the idea that God created me – perfect in design – and had blessed me with all authority and power to do *my thing* according to His Will for me. He had done that long before I knew. He did the same for you. That is a powerful thing to know and believe. So, believe that…

I watch these ministers, in particular, because they help me to get clarity about my life situations, consistently help me to keep my perspective in a healthy, spiritually grounded place, and help me to remember to trust God. They reaffirm that God is moving and leading me perfectly – every step of the way!

I need continuous inspiration and encouragement, so I read a lot of books that provide practical approaches and strategies to encourage myself when I need it. I am always looking for new tools to put into my tool box, as weaponry against negative thoughts that emerge to distract and discourage. I read books on personal growth and spiritual development to support my ability to see myself with an accurate perspective. I have gained a great deal of insight from authors like John C. Maxwell (*"How Successful People Think"*), Joyce Meyers (*"Eat the Cookie, Buy the Shoes"*, *"Do It Afraid"*), Max Lucado (*"Imagine Your Life Without Fear"*), Stephen Covey (*"The Speed of Trust"*), Rhonda Byrne (*"The Secret"*), Iyanla Vanzant (her complete works), and Bishop Jakes (anything written, on video or audio). These folks have introduced ideas that changed my thinking throughout the course of my recovery. And lately, I've become increasingly fond of writings outlined in the King James book of knowledge.

Another Thought....

As a Life Coach, Family Recovery Counselor, Master Educator and Licensed Social Worker, I am always working to help people to find solutions for themselves. So, in addition to my experience living according to recovery principles, I have included a practical guide that can be used in your daily living, to help you to deal with feelings of stress, worry and emotional uneasiness The next section is an excerpt from an informational guide to improve the state of your mental health, and to restore a sense of emotional equilibrium.

Hey, you've read this far. Don't stop now.…

This information is excerpted from the U.S. Department of Health and Human Services (DHHS), Substance Abuse & Mental Health Services Administration (SAMHSA), Center for Mental Health Services' **Action Planning for Prevention and Recovery: A Self-help Guide [to Recovering Your Mental Health].**

This segment contains information, ideas, and strategies that people have found to be helpful in relieving and preventing troubling feelings and symptoms. It includes information on "Developing a Wellness Toolbox", "Daily Maintenance Plan", "Early Warning", "When Things Are Breaking Down or Getting Worse", "Crisis Planning", and "Using Your Action Plans".

You may want to read through the entire excerpt before you begin working on developing an action plan for prevention and recovery. This can help enhance your understanding of the process of recovery. Work on each section. You may want to do this slowly, working on a portion of it, putting it aside, and revising it as you learn new things about yourself. Use it to identify ways that help you to feel better.

Introduction

Do you experience feelings that are upsetting, that keep you from being the way you want to be and doing things you want to do? Many people have troubling emotional, psychiatric or physical symptoms, and have made great advances in learning how to do things to get well and stay well. One of the most frustrating stages of recovering your health is when you realize that you can do things to help yourself stay well, but you can't figure out how to do them regularly. It is easy to forget simple things, especially when you're under stress or your issues begin to flare up.

The action plans for prevention and recovery described in this book were devised by people who have experienced emotional symptoms. They have developed ways to deal with the need for structure in their lives, ways that actively support their health. The plans are simple and can be changed over time, as you learn more about what you need to address. Anyone can use these plans for any kind of mental health concern. Those using these suggested methods report that by being prepared and taking action as necessary, they feel better more often and have improved the overall quality of their lives. One person said, "Finally, there's something I can do to help myself."

Action plans for prevention and recovery work because they:

- ❖ Are easy to develop and easy to use.
- ❖ Are individualized. You develop a plan for yourself. No one else can do it for you; however, you can reach out to others for assistance and support.
- ❖ Improve your ability to communicate effectively with your family members and health care providers
- ❖ Directly address the feelings, symptoms, circumstances, and events that are troubling you with plans to respond to them
- ❖ Renew your sense of hope that things can and will get better, and that you have control over your life and the way you feel.

Action Planning for Prevention and Recovery

Developing a Wellness Toolbox

To develop this plan, the only materials you need are a three-ring binder, a set of five tabs or dividers, and lined three-hole paper. Before you begin working with the tabbed sections, you will create a resource list to keep in the beginning of your binder. <u>This section is called the Wellness Toolbox</u>.

In the Wellness Toolbox, you will identify and list the things you use to help yourself feel better when you are having a hard time. Some of them are things you know you must do, like eating healthy meals and drinking plenty of water; others are things you could choose to do to help yourself feel better. You can also list things you would like to try using to keep yourself well or to help yourself feel better. You will refer to this list for ideas when you are developing the tabbed sections of your plan.

Some ideas for your Wellness Toolbox might be:

- Eating three healthy meals a day
- Drinking plenty of water
- Getting to bed by 10:00 p.m. (or at a good time for you)
- Doing something you enjoy – like playing an instrument, watching a favorite TV show, knitting, or reading a good book
- Exercising
- Doing a relaxation exercise
- Writing in your journal
- Talking to a friend on the telephone
- Taking vitamins and other food supplements
- Taking prescribed medications

You can get more ideas for your Wellness Toolbox by noticing good things you do as you go through your day, by asking your friends and family members for suggestions, and by looking for self-help resource books. Write down everything, from really easily accessible things, like taking deep breaths, to things you only do once in a while, like getting a massage. This is a resource list for you to refer back to when you are developing your plans. Your Wellness Toolbox works best if you have enough entries and feel you have an abundance of choices.

Just how many entries you record is up to you. If you feel positive and hopeful when you look at the list, then you have enough. You can continue to refine your Wellness Toolbox over time, adding to your list whenever you get an idea of something you'd like to try, and crossing things off your list if you find they no longer work for you.

Once you've gotten your Wellness Toolbox underway, insert it into your notebook. Then, insert your five tabbed dividers, with several sheets of paper after each tab and a supply of paper at the end of the notebook.

Daily Maintenance Plan

On the first tab, write "Daily Maintenance Plan." If you haven't done so, insert it in the binder along with several sheets of paper.

Feeling Well

On the first page, describe yourself when you are feeling all right. If you can't remember, or don't know how you feel when you are well, describe how you would like to feel. Make it easy. Make a list. Some descriptive words that are used include talkative, outgoing, energetic, humorous, or argumentative. When you aren't feeling very well, you can refer back to the list of things that outline how you want to feel.

Dreams and Goals

Some people use their plans to make a list of their dreams and goals. If you think you would find it helpful, make a list of goals you could work toward. You can write down long-term goals or those that are short-term and more easily achievable. It is really helpful to remember your dreams and goals, so you have something to look forward to. Then, you can identify steps to take to achieve them and incorporate these small steps into your daily maintenance plan.

Daily Maintenance List

On the next pages, describe those things you need to do every day to maintain your wellness. Use your Wellness Toolbox for ideas. Writing these things down, and reminding yourself daily to do them is an important step toward wellness. When you start to feel "out of sorts," you can often trace it back to "not doing" something on this list. Make sure you don't put so many things on this list that you can't possibly do them all. Remember, this is a list of things you must do, not things you may choose to do.

The following is a <u>sample</u> daily maintenance list:

- ❖ Eat three healthy meals and three healthy snacks that include whole grain foods, vegetables, and small portions of protein
- ❖ Drink at least six 8-ounce glasses of water
- ❖ Get exposure to outdoor light for at least 30 minutes
- ❖ Take medications and vitamin supplements
- ❖ Have 20 minutes of relaxation or meditation time or write in my journal for at least 15 minutes
- ❖ Spend at least ½ hour with a fun, affirming, or creative activity
- ❖ Check in with my partner for at least 10 minutes
- ❖ Check in with myself: "how am I doing physically, emotionally, and spiritually?"
- ❖ Go to work if it's a workday

Reminder List

On the next page, make a reminder list for yourself of things you might need to do. Check the list each day to ensure that you do those things that you need to do to keep yourself well. You will avoid a lot of stress that comes from forgetting occasional but important tasks.

Write "Do I Need To?" at the top of the page, and list things such as:

❖ Set up an appointment with a health care professional
❖ Spend time with a good friend or be in touch with my family
❖ Engage in peer counseling activity
❖ Do some housework
❖ Buy groceries
❖ Do the laundry
❖ Have some personal time
❖ Plan something fun for the evening or weekend
❖ Write some letters
❖ Go to a support group

That's the first section of the book. Cross out items if they stop working for you, and add new items as you think of them. You can even tear out whole pages and create new ones. You will be surprised how much better you will feel after taking some of these positive steps for yourself.

Triggers

Triggers are external events, situations or circumstances that can produce uncomfortable emotional symptoms, such as anxiety, panic, discouragement, despair, or negative self-talk. Reacting to triggers is normal, but if we don't recognize and respond to them appropriately, they may actually cause a downward spiral, making us feel worse. This section of your plan is meant to help you become more aware of your triggers and to help you develop plans to avoid or better handle triggering events. This will increase your ability to cope and stave off more severe symptoms.

Identifying Triggers

Write "Triggers" on the second tab and insert several sheets of paper. On the first page, write down those things that, if they occur, may cause an increase in your *symptoms*. They may have triggered or increased your symptoms in the past. It may be hard to think of every trigger right away. Add triggers to your list whenever you become aware of them. It is not necessary to project catastrophic things that might happen, such as war, natural disaster, or a huge personal loss. If those things were to occur, you would use the actions you describe in the triggers action plan more often and increase the length of time you engage in those activities. When listing your triggers, write those that are probable to occur, or may already be occurring in your life.

Some examples of common triggers are:

- ❖ The anniversary dates of losses or trauma

* Frightening, fear-provoking news events
* Too much to do and feeling overwhelmed
* Family friction or conflict
* The end of a relationship
* Spending too much time alone
* Being judged, criticized, teased, or put down
* Financial problems, getting a big bill
* Physical illness
* Sexual harassment
* Aggressive-sounding noises or exposure to anything that makes you feel uncomfortable
* Being around someone who has treated you badly
* Certain smells, tastes, or noises

Triggers Action Plan

On the next page, develop a plan of what actions you can take, if a trigger occurs, to comfort yourself and keep reactions from becoming more serious symptoms. Include tools that have worked for you in the past, use ideas you have learned from others, and refer back to your Wellness Toolbox. You may want to include things you must do at these times, <u>and</u> things you could do if you think those things may be helpful in the situation.

Your plan might include:

* Make sure I do everything on my daily maintenance list
* Call a support person and ask them to listen while I talk through the situation
* Pray

- ❖ Do a ½-hour relaxation exercise
- ❖ Write in my journal for at least ½-hour
- ❖ Ride my bicycle or exercise for 45 minutes
- ❖ Play the piano or work on a relaxing activity for 1 hour

If you do these things when you are triggered, and find them to be helpful, keep them on your list. If they are somewhat helpful, you may want to revise your action plan. If they are not helpful, remove them from your list and keep trying new ideas until you determine which are most helpful. You can learn about new tools by attending classes, workshops and lectures, reading self-help books, and talking to other people who experience similar symptoms. You should also be aware of the times when you need to contact your health care provider for support or assistance.

Early Warning Signs

Early warning signs are internal and may or may not arise in reaction to stressful situations. In spite of your best efforts, you may begin to experience early warning signs, those subtle signs that indicate that you may need to take further action. If you can recognize and address early warning signs right away, you may be able to prevent more severe symptoms. Reviewing early warning signs regularly can help you to become aware and prepared to circumvent them.

Write "Early Warning Signs" on the third tab and insert several more sheets of paper in your binder.

Identify Early Warning Signs

On the first page, make a list of early warning signs you have noticed in the past. How do you feel when you know you are not feeling quite right? How did you feel just before you had a hard time in the past? How did you feel when you noticed that habits or routines changed?

Your early warning signs might include things such as:

- Anxiety
- Nervousness
- Forgetfulness
- Inability to experience pleasure
- Lack of motivation
- Feeling slowed down or speeded up
- Being uncaring toward yourself or others
- Avoiding others or isolating
- Being obsessed with something that doesn't really matter
- Displaying irrational thought patterns
- Feeling unconnected to my body
- Increased irritability
- Increased negativity
- Not keeping appointments
- Changes in appetite
- Restlessness

If you want, ask your friends, family members and other supporters to discuss early warning signs that they've noticed for themselves. On the next pages, develop an action plan for responding to all identified early warning signs. Refer to your Wellness Toolbox for ideas. Some things you list may be the same as those you wrote on your Triggers Action Plan. If you notice this, be sure to prepare while you can.

The following is a sample plan to manage early warning signs:

- ❖ Do the things on my daily maintenance plan, whether I feel like it or not
- ❖ Tell a supporter/counselor how I am feeling and ask for advice. Ask him or her to help me figure out what action to take
- ❖ Engage in Peer counseling at least once each day
- ❖ Do at least three 10-minute relaxation exercises each day (simple exercises described in many self-help books that help you to relax, by focusing your attention on certain things)
- ❖ Write in my journal for at least 15 minutes each day
- ❖ Spend at least 1 hour involved in an activity I enjoy
- ❖ Ask others to handle my household responsibilities for a day
- ❖ Check in with my physician or other health care professional
- ❖ Read a good book
- ❖ Dance, sing, listen to good music, play an instrument, exercise

Again, if you use this plan and it doesn't help you feel better, revise your plan or create a new one. Use your Wellness Toolbox and other ideas from workshops, self-help books, your health care providers, and other people who deal with similar symptoms.

When Things Are Breaking Down or Getting Worse

In spite of your best efforts, your symptoms may progress to the point where they are uncomfortable, serious, and even dangerous. This is a very important time. It is necessary to take immediate action to prevent a crisis or loss of control. You may be feeling badly and others may be concerned for your wellness or safety. But you can still do things that you need to do to feel better and to be safe.

Write "When Things are Breaking Down" [or write something that means 'things are breaking down' to you] on the fourth tab. On the first page, make a list of symptoms that indicate to you that things are breaking down or getting worse.

Remember that symptoms and signs may vary from person to person. What may mean "things are getting much worse" to one person may mean a crisis to another. Signs or symptoms that things are breaking down might include:

- ❖ Feeling very oversensitive and fragile
- ❖ Responding irrationally to events and the actions of others
- ❖ Feeling very needy
- ❖ Being unable to sleep
- ❖ Sleeping all the time
- ❖ Avoiding eating or eating too much
- ❖ Wanting to be totally alone
- ❖ Chain smoking
- ❖ Substance (alcohol or other drug) abuse
- ❖ Taking out anger on others

On the next page, write an action plan that you think will help reduce your symptoms when they have progressed to this point.

<u>At this point, the plan needs to be very direct, with a limited number of choices and very clear instructions</u>.

Some ideas to include in your action plan might be:

- ❖ Call my doctor or other health care professional - ask for and follow his / her instructions
- ❖ Call and talk to my supporters for as long as necessary
- ❖ Arrange for someone to stay with me until symptoms subside
- ❖ Make arrangements to get help right away if my symptoms worsen
- ❖ Make sure I am doing everything on my daily check list
- ❖ Arrange and take a few days off from any responsibilities
- ❖ Have at least two Peer Counseling sessions
- ❖ Do deep-breathing relaxation exercises
- ❖ Write in my journal for at least ½-hour
- ❖ Schedule a physical examination or doctor's appointment or plan a consultation with a health care professional
- ❖ Ask to have current medication regimen reviewed

As with the other plans, make note of the parts of the plan that work especially well. If something doesn't work or doesn't produce desired outcomes, develop a different plan or revise the one that you used — when you are feeling better. Always look for new tools that can help you through these difficult situations.

Crisis Planning

Identifying and responding to symptoms early will reduce the chances that you will find yourself in a crisis. It is important to confront the potential for crisis, because <u>in spite of the best planning of effective actions, you could find yourself in a situation wherein others will need to take over responsibility for your care.</u>

Crisis is a difficult situation. In a crisis, you may feel as if you have lost control. Writing a crisis plan when you are feeling well, to provide instructions to others on how to care for you when you're not feeling well, will help you to maintain responsibility for your own care.

It will keep your family members and friends from wasting time trying to figure out what to do for you. It can relieve the guilt or feelings that family, friends or other caregivers can develop, if ill-prepared to take the correct actions on your behalf. A crisis plan can also ensure that your needs are met in the time of crisis, and that you will have better chances to get better as quickly as possible.

You must develop a crisis plan when you are feeling well. You must take adequate time, give deep thought, and determine appropriate collaborations that need to be arranged with health care providers, family members and other supporters.

Over the next few pages, information and ideas that others have included in their crisis plans will be shared. These ideas can help you to develop your own detailed crisis plan.

The Crisis Plan differs from the other action plans because <u>it will be used by others</u> to help you while in crisis.

The other four sections of this planning process are implemented by solely by you and need not be shared with anyone else. However, when writing a crisis plan, you must make it clear, easy to understand, and make sure that it is legible. While you may have developed other plans rather quickly, this plan is likely to take more time. <u>Don't rush the process.</u> Work at it for a while. Complete it and put it down for a few days. Continue to come back to it until you have developed a plan that you feel addresses all facets of a crisis situation, and has the best chance of working for you. Once you have completed your crisis plan, give copies to the people you name in the plan as supporters.

On the fifth tab write "Crisis Plan" and insert at least nine sheets of paper. The following sample crisis plan has nine parts: each part will address a particular concern.

Part 1: Feeling well

Write what you are like when you are feeling well. You can copy it from Section 1, Daily Maintenance Plan. This can help educate people who might be trying to help you. It might also help someone who knows you well to understand you a little better. For someone who doesn't know you, it is important to detail your description of you.

Part 2: Symptoms

Describe symptoms that would indicate to others that it is time for them to take over responsibility for your care and/or make decisions on your behalf. This will be hard for everyone. No one likes to think about someone taking responsibility for his/her care. Yet, through **a carefully developed description of symptoms that you know indicate that you can't make good decisions anymore, you can decide what happens for you, even when things are not in your control.**

Allow yourself plenty of time to complete this section. Ask your friends, family members, and other supporters for input, but always remember that the final decisions about your care are up to you. Be clear and specific in describing each symptom. Don't just summarize, use as many descriptive words as are needed.

Your list of symptoms might include—

- ❖ Being unable to recognize or identify family and friends
- ❖ Uncontrollable pacing; inability to stay still
- ❖ Neglecting personal hygiene for _____ (list how many days)
- ❖ Not cooking or doing housework _____ (list how many days)
- ❖ Not understanding what people are saying
- ❖ Thinking I am someone who I am not
- ❖ Thinking I have the ability to do something and I don't

- ❖ Displaying abusive, destructive, or violent behavior toward self, others or property
- ❖ Abusing alcohol and/or drugs
- ❖ Not getting out of bed _____ (list how many days)
- ❖ Refusing to eat or drink

Part 3: Supporters

In this next section of the crisis plan, list the people who you want to take over for you when symptoms listed in the previous section arise. Before listing people in this part of your plan, talk with them about what you'd like for them to do, and make sure they understand <u>and</u> agree to be in the plan.

Supporters can be family members, friends, or health care providers. They should be committed to adhering to plans as you have written them. When you first develop this plan, your list may be mostly health care providers. But as you work on developing your support system, try to add family members and friends who will be available to handle the responsibilities as outlined.

It's best to have at least five people on your list of supporters. If you have only one or two individuals, they may not be available when you need them. If you don't have many supporters now, you may need to work on developing new and/or closer relationships with people. Ask yourself about the best way to build these kinds of relationships. Seek new friends by doing different things, such as volunteering or going to support groups and community activities.

In the past, health care providers or family members may have made decisions that were not according to your wishes. You may not want them involved in your care again. If so, write on your plan, "I do not want the following people involved --- in any way --- in my care, my treatment, or decisions regarding such." Then list those people and describe why you don't want them involved in your care. They may be people who, in the past, have treated you badly, or have made poor decisions, or who get overly upset when you are having a hard time.

Many people like to include a section that describes how they want possible disputes over care, between the team of supporters, to be settled. For instance, you may want to state that if a disagreement occurs about a course of action, a majority of your supporters can decide or a particular person will make the final determination. You also may want to request that a consumer or advocacy organization becomes involved in the decision-making, if the need arises.

Part 4: Health Care Providers and Medications

List your physician, pharmacist, and other health care providers or professionals, and their phone numbers. Then list the following —

❖ The medications you are currently using, the dosage, and why you are using them
❖ The medications you would prefer to take if medications or additional medications become necessary (like those that have worked well for you in the past), and why you chose them

❖ The medications that would be acceptable if medications become necessary, and why you chose those medications
❖ The medications that must be avoided (because you are allergic to them, or they conflict with another medication, or they cause undesirable side effects) —give the reasons why they should be avoided.

List any vitamins, herbs, alternative medications (e.g. homeopathic remedies), and/or supplements you are taking. Note which of these should be increased or decreased if you are in crisis, and which you have discovered are not good for you.

Part 5: Treatments

There may be particular treatments that you like in a crisis situation and others that you would want to avoid. The reason may be as simple as "this treatment has or has not worked in the past," or you may have concerns about the safety of the treatment. Maybe you just don't like the way a particular treatment makes you feel. Treatments can mean a medical procedure or alternative therapy options, (such as injections of B vitamins, massages, or cranial sacral therapy).

In this part of your crisis plan, list the following:

• Treatments you are currently undergoing and why
• Treatments you would prefer if treatments or additional treatments became necessary and why you chose them

- Treatments that would be acceptable to you if treatments were deemed necessary by your support team
- Treatments that must be avoided and the reasons why

Part 6: Planning for Your Care

<u>Describe a plan for your care in a crisis that would allow you to stay where you want to stay.</u> Think about your family and friends. Would they be able to take turns providing care? Could transportation be arranged to health care appointments? Is there a program in your community that could provide you with care part of the time, with family members and friends taking care of you the rest of the time? Many people who prefer to stay at home rather than be hospitalized are setting up these kinds of plans.

You may need to ask your family members, friends, and health care providers what options are available. If you are having a hard time coming up with a plan, at least write down what you imagine the ideal scenario for you would be.

Part 7: Treatment Facilities

<u>Describe the treatment facilities you would like to use if family members and friends cannot provide you with care, or if your condition requires hospital care.</u> Your options may be limited by the facilities available in your area and by your health insurance coverage. If you are not sure which facilities you would like to use, write down a description of what the ideal facility would be like. Then, talk to family members and friends about the available choices. Call those

facilities to request information that can help you in making your decisions. Also include a list of treatment facilities you would like to avoid—such as places where you received poor care or treatment in the past.

Part 8: What You Need From Others

<u>Describe what your supporters can do for you that will help you feel better.</u> This part of the plan is very important and deserves careful attention. Describe everything you can think of that you want your family, friends and supporters to do (or not do) for you. You may get more ideas from supporters and health care professionals.

Things others could do to help you be more comfortable may include:

- ❖ Listen to me without giving me advice, judging me, or criticizing
- ❖ Hold me (how? How firmly? How long?)
- ❖ Let me pace
- ❖ Encourage me to move, help me move
- ❖ Lead me through a relaxation or stress reduction technique
- ❖ Provide Peer counseling to me
- ❖ Provide me with materials so I can draw or paint
- ❖ Give me the space to express my feelings
- ❖ Talk to me
- ❖ Don't talk to me
- ❖ Encourage me and reassure me

- ❖ Prepare nutritious foods; feed me the foods, if needed
- ❖ Make sure I take my vitamins and other medications
- ❖ Play videos (list what type of videos)
- ❖ Play good music (list what type of music)
- ❖ Let me rest

Include a list of specific tasks you would want others to do for you, which tasks you want specific persons to do, and any other specific instructions they may need.

These tasks might include:

- ❖ Buying groceries
- ❖ Watering the plants
- ❖ Feeding the pets
- ❖ Taking care of the children
- ❖ Paying the bills
- ❖ Taking out the garbage or trash
- ❖ Doing the laundry

You may also want to include a list of things that you do not want others to do for you—things that they might do because they think it would be helpful, but that might be harmful or worsen the situation.

These things you don't want done may include:

- ❖ Forcing me to do anything, such as walking
- ❖ Scolding me
- ❖ Becoming impatient with me
- ❖ Taking away my cigarettes or coffee
- ❖ Talking continuously

Some people also include instructions in this section on how they want to be treated by their caregivers. These instructions may include statements such as "kindly, but firmly, tell me what you are going to do," "don't ask me to make any choices at this point," or "make sure to take my medications out of my top dresser drawer right away."

Part 9: Recognizing Recovery

In the last part of this plan, give your supporters information on how they will recognize when you have recovered enough to take care of yourself and they no longer need to use this plan.

Some examples are:

- ❖ When I am eating at least two meals a day
- ❖ When I am awake for six hours a day
- ❖ When I am taking care of my personal hygiene needs daily
- ❖ When I can carry on a good conversation
- ❖ When I can easily walk around the house

You have now completed your crisis plan. **Update it when you learn new information or change your mind about things. Be sure to date your crisis plan each time you change it and give revised copies to your supporters.**

You can help to ensure that your crisis plan will be followed by signing it in the presence of two witnesses. It will further increase its use if you appoint and name a durable power of attorney – a person who can legally make decisions for you if you are not able to make them for yourself. Since power of attorney documents vary from state to state, you cannot be sure how the plan will be followed. However, it is your best assurance that your wishes will be honored.

Using Your Action Plans

You have now completed your action plans for prevention and recovery. At first, you will need to spend 15-20 minutes each day reviewing your plans. People report that the morning, either before or after breakfast, is the best time to review the book. As you become familiar with your daily list, triggers, symptoms and plans, you will find the review process takes less time and that you will know how to respond without even referring to the book.

Begin with Section 1. Review the list of how you are if you are all right. If you are all right, do the things on your list of things you need to do every day to keep yourself well. Also refer to the page of things you may need to do to see if anything "rings a bell" with you. If it does, make a note to yourself to include it in your day. If you are not feeling well, review the other sections to see where the symptoms you are experiencing fit. Then follow the action plan you have designed.

For instance, if you feel very anxious and know that it is because one of your triggers happened, follow the plan in the triggers section. If there weren't any particular triggers, but you noticed some early warning signs, follow the plan you designed for that section. If you notice symptoms that indicate things are breaking down, follow the plan you developed there.

If you are in a crisis situation, the plans can help you to realize it so you can let your supporters know they should take over. However, in certain crisis situations, you may not be aware or willing to admit that you are in crisis. This is why having a strong team of supporters is so important. They will observe the symptoms you have reported and take over responsibility for your care, whether or not you are willing to admit you are in a crisis at that time.

Distributing your crisis plan to supporters and discussing it with them is essential to your safety and well-being.

You may want to take your plan or parts of your plan to a copy shop to get a reduced-size copy to carry in your pocket, purse, or glove compartment of your car. Then you can refer to the plan if triggers or symptoms come up when you are away from home.

If you are in crisis, get immediate help:

- Call 911
- National Suicide Prevention Hotline: 1-800-273-TALK (8255) for English, 1-888-628-9454 for Spanish
- HYPERLINK "https://www.thehotline.org/" National Domestic Violence Hotline: 1-800-799-7233 or text LOVEIS to 22522
- HYPERLINK "https://www.childhelp.org/hotline/" National Child Abuse Hotline: 1-800-4AChild (1-800-422-4453) or text 1-800-422-4453

- HYPERLINK "https://rainn.org/" National Sexual Assault Hotline: 1-800-656-HOPE (4673)
- HYPERLINK "https://www.veteranscrisisline.net/" Veteran's Crisis Line : 1-800-273-TALK (8255)
- The Eldercare Locator: 1-800-677-1116
- HYPERLINK "https://www.samhsa.gov/disaster-preparedness" Disaster Distress Helpline: CALL or TEXT 1-800-985-5990

Now, you may say, "Wow! That's way too deep for me. I don't need to do all of that." And you may not…. But, I learned something from experienced group members of recovery – "It is better to have and not need than to need and not have." So, if the suggestions provided in the *Action Planning* excerpt do not apply to your current situation, put it away where you can access it when you need it.

Almost Final Thought...

Over the years, I have saved quite a few magazines and articles with information that encourages and inspires me. The excerpt below is from a 2006 volume of Essence Magazine, written by Susan L. Taylor, in her editorial column, In the Spirit. It is called *I Promise Myself.* I want to share some of it with you, so you'll remember to be good to yourself, too.

"I didn't understand then that every crisis is a call from God — a summons to deep reflection, life-changing decision making and commitment to spiritual practice. I know this now.... I've promised myself to be accountable and responsible for who I am and what I want to become. My psyche and soul have suffered.... But, life is good; in each moment, we get to choose again. ...this is a time of transformation for you and me. Our awakening. It's our time to rise...time to reawaken a sureness of purpose within ourselves.... Whisper these few promises to your soul in the quiet of each morning — or create your own affirmations. This will create a sacred space for healing and inner cheering. It will help you honor the perfection God made and find and follow the divine-right path life has prepared for you:

I promise myself *to live by the authority of my own soul today and practice being my own best friend and motivator. I promise to speak to myself kindly and to give myself the attention and nourishment I need. I promise to remember that others' opinions judgments and deeds can't diminish me. I promise not to hide out or play it safe, but to bring my open heart and Master mind to each moment with confidence. I promise to believe in myself and in the genius of my people.*

I promise myself *to live this day with joy and enthusiasm, to allow only love and light to flow through me no matter who or what life sends my way. Everywhere I look I will see beauty and possibility, and I will let my light shine in service to my people, giving joyfully from a full cup.*

I promise myself *to remember that every circumstance is a pathway to God; that every crisis is temporary and lasts not a moment longer than it takes for me to surrender it to God and ask for a divine solution.*

I promise myself *to remain faithfully aware that God is always here, with and within me. That no matter what the question, God is the answer. No matter what the need, God is the fulfillment. I promise myself to remember."*

Now, these are words to live by....

I also want to share is something that a friend of mine shared at her celebration of clean time. When I recalled these words, I thought of how appropriate it would be to share these very inspirational words with you, as one of my closing thoughts.

This is an excerpt from "Today's Word with Joel and Victoria [Olsteen]" – a message sent daily to his subscribers:

"There may be old things in your life that you are trying to get rid of. Maybe you have old habits or addictions that you want to change. Remember today that the new has come. It's a new year with new opportunities, and it's time for you to be the new you. Let this be the year that you break old habits and addictions. Let this be the year that you move forward into a new life of victory. Let this be the year that you take hold of all the spiritual blessings that [God] has promised – peace, health, protection and victory. Be encouraged today because no matter what is happening in your life right now, you have a chance for a new beginning.

Choose today to leave the old behind – old behaviors, old thinking, old words – and embrace the new by faith because this is your year to experience the new life that He has prepared for you!

PRAYER FOR TODAY: "Thank you for making me new. I choose today to leave behind the old life and ask that you empower me by your spirit. Help me to understand Your Plan…"

I hope you are inspired and encouraged by these words.

Final Thought...

I hope this information helps you to begin your road to recovery from whatever it is that stands in your way, the distractions that prevent you from achieving all of the desires of your heart. I hope this book has ignited your flame, gassed up your engine, and serves to motivate, equip and inspire you to create the momentum needed to pursue the things that you deserve. Remind yourself that you deserve to have a life that you want.

BELIEVE THAT YOU CAN RECOVER FROM EVERYTHING!!

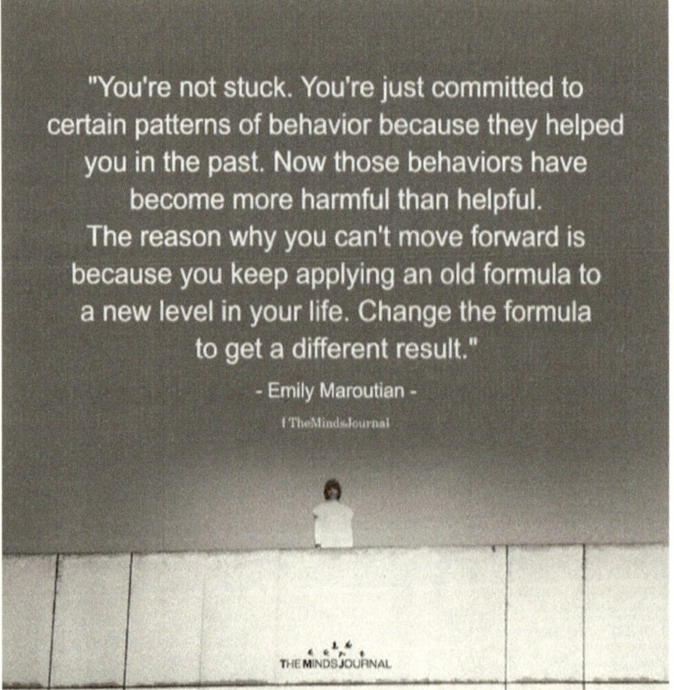

"You're not stuck. You're just committed to certain patterns of behavior because they helped you in the past. Now those behaviors have become more harmful than helpful.
The reason why you can't move forward is because you keep applying an old formula to a new level in your life. Change the formula to get a different result."
- Emily Maroutian -
f TheMindsJournal
THE MINDS JOURNAL

www.ingramcontent.com/pod-product-compliance
Lightning Source LLC
Chambersburg PA
CBHW022104050726
47591CB00002B/660